NEW IMAGES OF
MUSICAL SOUND

NEW IMAGES OF MUSICAL SOUND

Robert Cogan

HARVARD UNIVERSITY PRESS
Cambridge, Massachusetts
and London, England
1984

Copyright © 1984 by the President and Fellows of Harvard College
All rights reserved
Printed in the United States of America
10 9 8 7 6 5 4 3 2 1

This book is printed on acid-free paper, and its binding materials have
been chosen for strength and durability.

Library of Congress Cataloging in Publication Data

Cogan, Robert, 1930–
    New images of musical sound.

    Includes index.
    1. Music—Theory.   2. Music—Analysis, appreciation.
3. Sound.   I. Title.
MT6.C63N5   1984   781′.22′028   83-12998
ISBN 0-674-61585-9

Acknowledgments

The process for making the spectrum photos of complete musical contexts in this book was developed by Dale Teaney and his associate, Charles Potter, at the Watson Research Center of IBM. Without their professional and personal initiatives, the process would have become available to musicians much later than it did.

The work of developing an analytic theory of tone color in music has been shared with me for many years by Pozzi Escot, and has benefited from the contributions of many perceptive students in graduate seminars at New England Conservatory. Much of the theory in this book has its roots in *Sonic Design: The Nature of Sound and Music* (which Escot and I wrote in 1976) and was developed in those seminars. The spectrum photos were taken by me during the years 1980–81 in the Sonic Analysis Laboratory at New England Conservatory. I alone am responsible for any defects in them and for the theories developed around them.

In reading the manuscript as it evolved, Joseph Agassi, David Lewin, and Anne Chatoney Shreffler all have contributed valuable suggestions. Matthew Warnick stimulated several specific ideas in Part II. Chance encounters with Wayne Slawson at different stages of the writing revealed shared concerns, and struck many useful sparks even when our opinions diverged. Andrew Toth made available the Balinese *gendèr* analyzed in Chapter 2.

For assistance in the Sonic Analysis Laboratory, I am indebted as well to Frederick Mintzer and Antonio Ruiz of Watson Research Center, IBM; Robert Rachdorf and David Read of New England Conservatory; and George Hughes.

My editors, Maria Ascher, Joan Mark, and Elyse Topalian, have been everything an author could hope for.

Through science and technology, as well as through the continuing traditions of music theory, this book approaches large, heretofore open questions of tone color and structure in music. A musician uninterested in these matters seems to me almost a contradiction in terms. My own awareness grew enormously, in very different directions, as the result of early contact with Roger Sessions and Milton Babbitt. I would like to acknowledge here their diverse, invaluable contributions.

Contents

Introduction   1

Part I. Images of Sonic Structure

1. Voices   23

> Photo 1. Gregorian Chant: "Qui Sedes, Domine"
>
> Photo 2. Tibetan Tantric Chant: Invocation of Mahakala
>
> Photo 3. Billie Holiday: "Strange Fruit"
>
> Photo 4. Gyorgy Ligeti: *Lux Aeterna*

2. Instruments   44

> Photo 5. Balinese Shadow-play Music: *Pemoengkah*
>
> Photo 6. Ludwig van Beethoven: Piano Sonata in E, Opus 109, First Movement
>
> Photo 7. Igor Stravinsky: *Three Pieces for String Quartet,* Piece II
>
> Photo 8. Anton Webern: *Four Pieces for Violin and Piano,* Opus 7, Pieces III and IV
>
> Photo 9. Elliott Carter: *Eight Etudes and a Fantasy,* Etude III

3. Large Mixed Ensembles   73

> Photo 10. Wolfgang Amadeus Mozart: Requiem K. 626, "Confutatis"
>
> Photo 11. Hector Berlioz: Te Deum, "Tibi Omnes Angeli"
>
> Photo 12. Claude Debussy: Nocturnes, "Nuages"
>
> Photo 13. Alban Berg: *Wozzeck,* Act III, Scene 2
>
> Photo 14. Edgard Varèse: *Hyperprism*

4. Electronic and Tape Music   103

     Photo 15. Milton Babbitt: *Ensembles for Synthesizer*,
              Introduction
     Photo 16. Jean-Claude Risset: *Little Boy*, "Fall"
     Photo 17. Robert Cogan: *No Attack of Organic Metals*

Part II. Tone Color: A Phonological Theory

5. The Theory of Oppositions   123

6. Specific Oppositions   133

7. Parenthetical Issues   141

8. Archetypes   147

Conclusion   153

Appendix A. Spectral Analysis and Spectral Display   155
Appendix B. Tables of Oppositions   157
Notes   166
Index   174

Let the sense of hearing be excited, and from the lightest breath to the wildest din, from the simplest sound to the highest harmony, from the most vehement and impassioned cry to the gentlest word of reason, still it is Nature that speaks and manifests her presence, her power, her pervading life and the vastness of her relations.

—GOETHE, Preface to
The Theory of Color, 1810

Introduction

MUSIC IS SAID to be the art of sound. Stravinsky, for example, called his music speculations in "sound and time."[1] But what is musical sound? How do musical sounds combine to form musical contexts, tone colors and textures, and ultimately whole musical works? Sound in music has for millennia proved to be inscrutable—beyond description and analysis in almost every musical tradition. As his first example of the gap that separates our knowledge from our descriptive powers, the philosopher Wittgenstein chose "how a clarinet sounds."[2]

The very essence of a musical culture, epoch, or style is embodied in its unique sound. A familiar example is the historical epochs and styles of European classical music: the harpsichord- and continuo-dominated sonorities of the Baroque; the muted strings, flutes, and harps of Impressionism; or the brass and percussion of modernism. Entire cultures can be evoked by a single sonic cliché: a gong summons up the islands and mainland of Asia; ensembles of diverse drums, Africa. These are clichés of a special kind—signaling, at the same time, the familiar and the inexplicable. For to a surprising extent the sonic nature of cultures, historical epochs, particular styles, individual composers, and integral compositions all have been indecipherable to musicians. The sonic has remained outside—or only at the very edge of—musical analysis and discourse.

Some traditions, most notably that of European music theory inherited in North and South America, strive to reduce the complex information of musical sounds to *notes*. Notes, however, name only one aspect of a sound: a focal pitch, if and when one exists. Chinese of the Sung dynasty, sensitive to sonic qualities, bridged the gap between notes and sounds with poetic metaphors. One musical instrument sound was "dragonflies alighting on water"; another was "a cold cicada bemoaning the coming of autumn."[3] Although marvelously evocative, such images bring us no closer to sonic understanding—no closer, particularly, to the role of any sound in its sonic context.

Only now, through a new synthesis of scientific and musical analysis, can we begin to probe the sonic enigma. Photographs of the spectral formation of musical works provide a bridge that makes a new understanding of sound and music, sound *in* music, possible. The photographic images in this book are at present unique. They are the first to reveal the underlying spec-

Fig. 1. Segments of four spectrum photos. (a) Billie Holiday, "Strange Fruit" (Photo 3). (b) Beethoven, Piano Sonata in E Opus 109 (Photo 6). (c) Alban Berg, *Wozzeck*, Act III, Scene 2 (Photo 13). (d) Jean-Claude Risset, "Fall" (Photo 16).

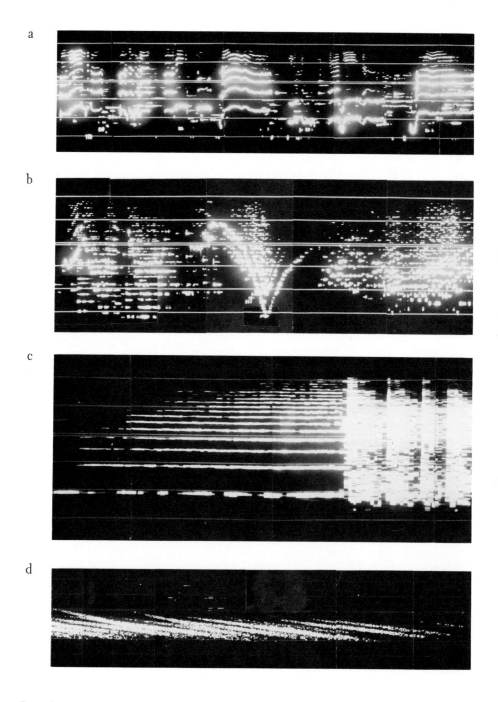

a

b

c

d

tral, sonic detail not of isolated single sounds (such photographs are not uncommon) but rather of entire musical works (or substantial segments of them) in a kind of X-ray or electron photographic display. They reveal a structural aspect of musical shapes and forms that until now has remained hidden (see Figure 1). They objectify much that has previously been most elusive, even mystifying, about sounds and the ways they create the design of musical structures. In so doing, they illuminate the very nature of musical structure and expression.

At a glance, the photo segments of Figure 1 make visible many significant aspects of the sonic formation of their musics. We instantly see the subtle note-bending inflections of Billie Holiday's singing, and the highly structured cascades of sonic elements of a Beethoven piano sonata. No less apparent is the violent intensity of oppositions in the sound spectrum at the climactic moment of murder in Berg's opera *Wozzeck*, or the drifting sonic dissolution that concludes Jean-Claude Risset's computer piece "Fall."

In hearing music we seem to perceive its sound, its tone colors, and its textures immediately and directly. At the same time, these qualities have been especially difficult to understand. Now, by means of spectrum photos, we find the constituent sonic details laid out with an impact that is almost as immediate and direct as the sounds they picture. This book is designed to illuminate, as fully and richly as possible, the meaning of those photos and of the sonic elements and contexts that they reveal.

In doing so, it makes use of the knowledge and methods of several fields. It combines analytic processes of music and of physics. It derives guidance from linguistics, where the analysis of language sounds has already led to discoveries whose implications go far beyond the field. The analyses are written in a style that should be accessible to musicians, scientists, or any others interested in those subjects. The aim is to use scientific and musical analysis to shed light on the essence of musical sound structures, not to erect additional technical barriers.

MUSIC, SOUND, AND IMAGE

Let us orient ourselves in the spectral world. We live in a sea of vibrations, ourselves vibrant within it; this is a central revelation of the science of the past hundred years. Light, colors, sound, electricity, even matter itself all exhibit wave-like properties, vibrating at one or more speeds, their *frequencies*. Depending upon their frequencies, we perceive wave vibrations as colors or sounds, radio waves, X-rays, or other spectral phenomena. Astronomers carry out spectrum analyses of the cosmos in order to discover wave traces of heavenly bodies and events—traces such as radio waves and cosmic rays. At the other end of the physical scale, physicists measure the vibration rates and resonances of the most minute subatomic units.

Analyzing the universe, scientists have learned that in daily life we see and touch only the surface of an almost unimaginable complexity. The ancient notion of *matter* has gradually been replaced by an intricate tracery of particles and waves, subatomic structures, electrical impulses, and mathematical concepts. Parallel to the universe that we see and touch exists a sonic universe that we hear. Beneath the surface of that sonic world, and in music beneath the surface of notes and instruments, there exists another world: that of sound waves, of overtones or partials that make up the sound spectrum, and of other minute, obscure phenomena. Sonic science has revealed that even so-called *single* sounds—a spoken vowel, for example, or a single note of a musical instrument—are almost always each a *complex* of diverse waves and vibrations, of multiple partials, and of a host of other sonic phenomena. This atomic-like sound spectral world creates, as its elements are combined, shaped, and structured, the surface of notes and instrumental sounds, musical formations, and musical works that we know. It is these atomic-like spectral features that the spectrum photos make visible, thus revealing the sonic structures that they form.

For musicians, news of this spectral level of sonic detail has often been a kind of rumor drifting toward them from the fields of physics, acoustics, psychoacoustics, and linguistics. It has been rumor not only because of the distance that usually separates scientists and musicians, but also because of the disjunct, fragmentary nature of the information: for example, information about the acoustic characteristics of a single isolated sound—a single note of a single instrument. The technical and conceptual limitation of early acoustic studies to single sounds removed from musical contexts rendered them difficult for musicians to absorb and use. Since music is not merely a single note of a single instrument, early acoustic studies left a wide gap between the information received and actual musical formations and experience. This book will try to make some essential connections—to link the most minute sonic phenomena to complete musical gestures and formations, the finest physical features to the fullest structural and expressive statements.

In one of the earliest-known considerations of the atom, Democritus said: "By convention there is color, by convention sweetness, by convention bitterness, but in reality there are atoms and space."[4] I am tempted to paraphrase Democritus—to say that in sonic reality "there are spectra and space." The temptation is especially strong now that the sound spectrum analyzer is able to reveal previously hidden spectral sonic elements.

Democritus, however, in his polemical enthusiasm countered one extreme with its opposite. Reality is neither exclusively the "psychological" attributes of color, sweetness, and bitterness nor the "physical" attributes of spectra and space. Reality, musical reality above all, is composed of many interacting levels and layers. Indeed, much of the essence of musical reality lies in the very meeting ground where spectra and space (as they manifest themselves in any given context) participate in forming our perceptions of musical color and music's expressive qualities—its "sweetness" and "bitterness."

In interpreting the spectrum photos, this book will explore that meeting ground. The commentaries that accompany the spectrum photos begin a process, probably not soon to be completed, of interpreting and understanding this level of sonic and musical shaping. They consider the ways in which the micro- and macroformations of musical works—their spectral details and their large motions—unite to create sonic character. Pozzi Escot and I called this meeting ground *sonic design.*[5] In referring to languages, Roman Jakobson, a leading analyst of linguistic sound, called it their *sound shape.*[6]

Spectrum photos display sonic formations vividly, but they do not quite speak for themselves (a tempting illusion). The commentaries, therefore, direct the reader's attention to those elements that are essential for an understanding of the photos—some of these elements prominent, many of them more subtle. The reader is invited to participate in considering the shaping of the sonic context of each musical work. To make this possible, information about sources (scores, recordings, and so forth) is provided.

In music, the spectral sonic details and structures come not directly from the creative musical imagination, but rather from the imagination as it speaks through the voices and instruments of performers. The most immediate sources of the spectral features are those voices and instruments, even if the instruments happen to be twentieth-century sound synthesizers and computers. In order to explore and reveal the spectral resources offered by diverse sonic media, the works analyzed have been divided into four groups (as in Figure 1): music for voices, for instruments, for large mixed ensembles, and for electronic tape. The music has been chosen from the widest possible range of media, historical epochs, and cultures; readers will see that although sound everywhere and always may have been inscrutable, it has also been expressive.

Seventeen spectrum photos with commentaries comprise Part I of this book. Part II considers in a more complete and formal way the significance of these new revelations for musical analysis and understanding. The sonic characteristics discovered in Part I become the basis of an explicit theory of tone color in music, of a process for analyzing and understanding tone color formations.

It is in Part II that connections with linguistic theory are most apparent. Even in Part I, musical sounds and language sounds interconnect—inescapably so in music for human singing voices that is based on languages. In such music there can be no complete, final separation of one sonic realm from the other; they blend into each other. Moreover, linguistics in the last fifty years has been concerned with the analysis of language sounds. Research in the field of linguistic phonology has revealed much about the sound shape of languages: the meanings, functions, and values of distinctive sonic features in creating the special sonic character of a particular language or linguistic utterance. We find many parallels (if not complete congruency) between musical and linguistic sound, and, more especially, we find in linguistic phonological analysis a stimulating model for defining sonic features and their interrelationships. The creation of sound shapes thus lies at the very core of languages and musics—sound shapes that in both domains now stand revealed by analysis.

This book, then, proceeds through two analytic stages. The first shows how to read the spectrum photos for their significant formations and details. The photos serve as a sonic "fingerprint," often as distinctive for a given genre, period of music, or composer as a fingerprint is for a person. The discussion explores the meanings of the sonic distinctions that emerge from the spectral fingerprint—for example, from Holiday's note-bendings, Beethoven's cascading elements, Berg's dramatic oppositions, or Risset's dissolving features. The second stage generalizes about the available sonic distinctions and about the sonic transformation and structuring processes.

Ultimately it will be possible to suggest, sometimes even to state, how the musical sound of one culture, composer, or work compares with the musical sound of another. A consideration of these spectrum photos and of their corresponding musical works leads to a marvelous realization: that musical works, despite their great diversity of origins and media, are in fact specific, concrete shapings and formations, rather than mere scatterings, of the basic sonic *stuff*. Musicians—composers and performers—in almost every musical culture and historical epoch, often unconsciously, have shaped sonic features into patterns and structures; these can now be seen, analyzed, and understood. From such analyses, which are only just beginning, new discoveries about the nature of music and the human sonic world will continue to emerge. It has been a rare privilege to have been among the first to glimpse this vista—to watch these levels of musical reality appear in all their variety, complexity, and sheer substantiality in these unique photographs and in the research they have inspired.

VIEWING SPECTRUM PHOTOS

Spectrum photos make it possible to capture and examine the minute, changing elements that form and affect sonic reality. This section introduces basic sonic concepts necessary for viewing the photos. It is not meant to be technically exhaustive but to aid readers in discovering the wealth of sonic detail and in evaluating its possible significance. If they prefer, readers may explore the spectrum photos without advance preparation, feeling their way into the sonic patterns and designs (beginning in Part I).

Sound Waves. It is characteristic of waves that they repeat their pattern over and over. To human senses, wave repetitions can appear sometimes as sound, sometimes as light and color. Wave repetitions ranging from 15 per second to 20,000 per second are perceived as sound. Although such wave speeds might seem rapid, in fact they are among the slowest phenomena of the wave world. Light-wave repetitions range in speed from 10^{12} to 10^{15} per second, while radio, X-ray, gamma, and cosmic waves range from 10^{14} to 10^{20} per second.

In the case of sound waves, the slower the wave cycle the lower the sound—the faster the higher. Fifteen wave patterns, or cycles, per second (abbreviated *cps*—or *Hz*, for *Hertz*) is approximately the lowest audible

Fig. 2. The audible range, divided into registers and compared to a piano keyboard.

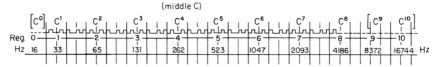

sound; 20,000 Hz is the highest. Figure 2 shows how these wave *frequencies* (also called, in music, *pitches* or *notes*) fall on, or outside, the common piano keyboard. (This figure is discussed further below.)

Humans do not directly perceive sound waves as a wave-like sensation: the human hearing mechanism translates the wave phenomenon into relatively steady sounds. It is the *speed of repetition* of the wave pattern that the human perceptual system responds to as frequency or pitch. Only when the *speed* of the wave repetitions changes do we perceive a pitch change. Mirroring human perception, the spectrum photos do not picture waves directly, but rather picture the *sound*, steady or changing, that results from the waves. For example, Figure 3 pictures a sound as it ascends through much of the audible range: its generating waves accelerate from 131 to 4,186 Hz (from C^3 to C^8).

Musical Space. As Figure 3 shows, the spatial orientation of the spectrum photos mirrors that of our hearing: lower sounds appear lower in the picture space; higher sounds appear higher.

Musical space has often been conceived of not merely as having different regions, lower and higher, and different directions, ascending and descending; it has also been described as comprising different octave *registers* that reproduce, lower or higher, the same relationships (for example, the same recurring scalar notes C, D, E, F, G, A, and B). The audible range

Fig. 3. Spectrum of a sine-tone sweep through registers 3–7.

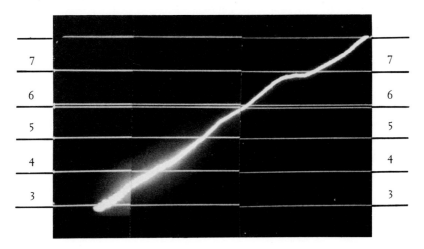

of humans encompasses approximately ten such registers. The registers can be numbered, as Figure 2 shows, according to international acoustic practice: middle C is C^4; its register, register 4, includes all sounds up to the next higher C, C^5, which begins register 5; and so forth. The modern piano covers registers 1 through 7 entirely; its lowest C is C^1, and its highest is C^8.

Each spectrum photo covers at least five contiguous registers, and sometimes more; these are indicated by the numbers at the left and right edges (see Figure 3). For each photo those registers have been chosen that include the greatest amount of spectral detail: they show the field of spectral action for any given sonic medium and musical work. In many of the photos, thin white horizontal lines extend across the entire picture. These horizontals mark the registral boundaries, falling between the note B in one register and C in the next higher register. A double line of this kind appears at 1,000 Hz, between B^5 and C^6. With practice, one can learn to estimate any note by its relative placement within a register.

The spectrum analyzer that produced these analyses can focus on any five contiguous registers at one time. The limitation to a five-register range, approximately half the human audible range, might seem restrictive. In many contexts, however, that turns out to be the range of significant sonic action. Where it is not, the analytical range has been expanded by taking two sets of photos—one focused on the lower registers, the other on the higher—and combining them. Consequently, some of the photos cover a range larger than five octaves.

Within each register the spectrum analyzer is not limited to the twelve-fold tempered division of the piano keyboard. Since it can make finer distinctions, the photos can picture continuum-like formations such as note bending, slides, or dense noise bands. The photographic representation is always somewhat thicker for lower-register sounds (in the lower half of the photos) than for higher-register sounds (see Figure 3).

Musical Time. In the spectrum photos, time is represented horizontally. The duration represented by each photo, ranging from 27 seconds to 11 minutes 22 seconds, is given in the commentaries. The time scale of the photos can be varied, allowing for the representation in each case of more, or less, sonic detail. Within a photo the time scale, of course, remains constant.

In selecting the time scale for a photo, the aim has been to represent a musical work, or a substantial segment of one, as a sonic (and visual) whole. In this way, the significance of any sonic detail can be assessed, as it must be, in relation to its sonic context. The layout of each photo is designed to clarify the musical structure as it unfolds in time. Each line of a photo represents a section, or other meaningful segment, of a total structure.

Occasionally it has been useful to picture a particular sound spectrum outside the flow of musical time and outside its full context, merely as a single isolated sonic moment. A number of such pictures, called *details*, are shown in the following pages.

Spectra. At the core of this study lies the sound spectrum. What exactly is it, and why does it occupy the center of our attention?

It has dawned only gradually on musicians and scientists that most sounds usually regarded as *single* are actually sonic compounds or complexes. Most sounds, whether a single-seeming element of spoken language (a vowel or a consonant), or of a single-seeming note played by a single musical instrument, are actually multiplex.

The reason for their multiple elements is quite simple. Vibrating bodies (a taut string, for example) vibrate simultaneously as a whole and *in parts*. The smaller parts of the body vibrate faster than the larger whole, their faster frequencies producing higher sounds than the slower fundamental vibrations of the whole body. The faster, higher vibrations are called *overtones* or *partials*, after the partial vibrations that produce them. Such multiple vibrations are produced by the strings of pianos, guitars, violins, and other stringed instruments, as well as by vocal cords; also by the reeds and air columns of wind instruments; and even by the skins and metal plates of percussion instruments.

An unsophisticated viewer of Figure 1 might imagine that the multiple simultaneous spectral strands of any photo segment originate from many voices or instruments combined, whereas they often originate in the spectral complexity of a *single* note by a *single* voice or instrument. In Figure 1c, for example, the initial two-thirds of the photo is dominated by a long crescendo of the single note, B^3, the lowest horizontal strand. All of the higher horizontals are upper partials of that fundamental. Furthermore, the great vertical swaths that complete Figure 1c are each caused by a single stroke on a single bass drum. A single note, a single voice sound, or a single instrumental stroke can generate numerous spectral pitches scattered throughout the audible range. *The sound spectrum is the total result of all the vibrations, fundamental and partial. It includes all of the sounding elements that, together, make any sonic impression.*

Although earlier scientists had become aware of the presence of partials, it was Hermann von Helmholtz, in the 1860s, who revolutionized sonic understanding by equating the tone color (or quality) of any sound with the spectral elements that compose it.[7] A shrill sound would reveal more, and stronger, high partials, whereas a duller sound would reveal fewer, if any, of them. For example, shriller vowels like [ɛ] (eh) and [i] (ee) are distinguished from more mellow vowels like [a] (ah) and [u] (oo) by their higher spectral partials (see Figures 4 and 5).[8] An oboe is distinguishable from a flute in a similar way, when both instruments play the same note. Since Helmholtz, it has become increasingly clear that to understand the sonic phenomena of language and music, one must understand the function of those spectral presences.

On the basis of their spectral formation, we can divide sounds into three very general categories. The first category consists of a sound that comprises *only* a fundamental, with no upper partials or other spectral elements. This sound, comparatively rare among real sounds, is called a *sine tone*, named

Fig. 4. Spectra of four sung vowels, taken from Photo 1 ("Qui sedes, Domine").

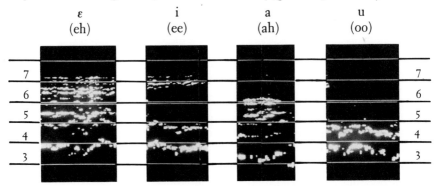

Fig. 5. Spectral detail of four vowels spoken by a woman. In details, each spike indicates a partial; the height indicates its relative intensity.

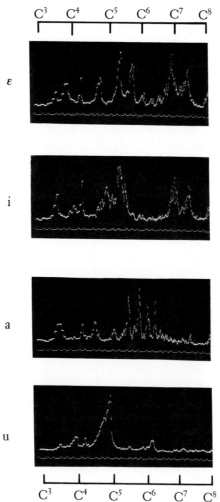

after the sine-shaped wave that produces it. Its simple spectrum is seen in Figure 3; nowhere during the ascending sweep is anything but the fundamental heard or seen.

The second category consists of those sounds whose spectrum is *harmonic* in relation to the fundamental tone. In a harmonic spectrum, the frequencies of the partials, or overtones, are whole-number multiples of the frequency of the fundamental. For example, the first ten partials of C^3, 131 Hz, are:

131	262	393	524	655	786	917	1,048	1,179	1,310
1	2	3	4	5	6	7	8	9	10
C^3	C^4	G^4	C^5	E^5	G^5	B^{b5}	C^6	D^6	E^6

(The notes indicated are the closest tempered notes to the indicated frequencies.) As a body vibrates at one-half, one-third, one-quarter, and so forth of its total length, it produces the indicated series of upper partials. That vibrating bodies behave in this complex way may seem odd, but it is actually very common. A vocal cord or stringed instrument can produce twenty or more harmonic partials at once in this way, as the string vibrates as a whole and in its fractional parts simultaneously.

What is especially noteworthy about harmonic spectra is the way they reinforce their fundamental frequency. In the example just shown, 131 is not only the wave frequency of the fundamental but is also the distance separating each successive partial. Consequently, it is reinforced with the appearance of every successive partial. The ear responds to this multiple reinforcement by hearing the spectrum as if it were a single note, the fundamental. Such spectra, which convey the illusion of being single notes, are characteristic of what we call a *pitched* musical instrument. In language, harmonic spectra are characteristic of vowels.

As described above, the harmonic spectrum is an abstraction: it represents *potentially* available subdivisions of vibrating bodies. Helmholtz gave concrete form to this abstraction by observing that the number and strength of harmonic partials vary in different musical instruments and their sounds, and that their tone colors change as a result. The vast diversity of tone colors of the world's pitched musical instruments depends, in part, upon their particular selection of partials made available in harmonic spectra.

Figure 1c shows a harmonic spectrum that gradually evolves in complexity as additional partials of the fundamental, B^3, gradually appear. Its particular pattern—individual strands more widely separated in the lower regions, less so in the higher regions—is characteristic of harmonic spectra. The spectral formation in this example is produced by all of the pitched instruments of an orchestra gradually joining in on the fundamental note, B^3.

The third category of spectra is typified by dense bands or swaths, such as those that immediately follow the strands of partials in Figure 1c. Dense spectral bands are characteristic of many of the sounds we call *noise*. Non-pitched percussion instruments in music, and consonants in language, frequently create such spectral bands. Their sounds activate not a single point in space, or even a discrete set of points, but rather one or more entire regions of musical space.

In addition to the particular category of spectral formation that makes up a given context, spectrum photos also show every participating spectral element—or at least every participating spectral element up to certain very fine limits of analysis, limits defined by both brevity and softness. The photos do not, however, give a precise rendering of the *intensity* (or loudness) of the spectral elements. Intensity can sometimes be inferred from the brightness, width, or constancy of a spectral image. However, the sonic cross-sections shown in the detail photos do reveal the relative intensities of the spectral elements of those chosen moments (see Figure 5 and the detail photos throughout).

Register. Shortly after Helmholtz's spectral breakthrough, the philosopher-scientist Ernst Mach made an important but little-recognized contribution to sonic analysis. As a result of his preoccupation with the perception of physical phenomena, Mach noticed a problem with Helmholtz's theory. Helmholtz believed that the tone color of all sine tones is uniform because—in his theory—their uniform spectrum determines their tone color. Mach, however, noticed that sine tones have *different* sonic qualities depending upon their register.[9] In the lowest registers a sine tone suggests the dull, grave sounds [u] (oo) or [o] (oh); in higher registers its quality resembles [a] (ah) or the bright, acute sound [i] (ee). The transformation of sine tone color by register can be approximately described as:

1–2	4	5	6	7	8
[u]	[o]	[a]	[e]	[I]	[i]
(oo)	(oh)	(ah)	(ey)	(ih)	(ee)

In view of the sine tone's spectral uniformity, how are its changes of quality from dark to bright or (according to linguistic terminology) from grave to acute to be explained? Mach concluded that register, like spectrum, must be a fundamental factor of tone color. Each register resembles a particular value, or coloration—darker or brighter. Sounds are not merely assemblages of spectral elements, as Helmholtz proposed, but assemblages of spectral elements located in specific registers. Placed in different registers, the same spectral recipe would produce a markedly different tone quality. Where the spectral recipe is a mixture of low-register spectral elements, the resulting compound reflects the duller [u]- and [o]-like colorations. Where it is a mixture of high-register spectral elements, the result is bright and [i]-like.

Mach's contribution has made the analysis of spectra even more concrete. Whereas Helmholtz had taken the abstraction of the harmonic series of partials and had shown that specific spectra present only certain partials in certain quantities, Mach demonstrated that those partials activate specific registral sonic qualities, depending on the registers in which they fall. Mixing partials in different registers means injecting specific quantities of the sonic character of each component's register into the total sonority. The spectrum photos reveal which registers are activated in a context and to what degree.

Because of the significance of registral color, no sonic preparation is more useful for reading the spectrum photos than carefully listening to a sine tone sweep through the entire audible range. One can clearly hear the changing coloration of the sine tone and the specific *value* of each register.

Every spectrum photo reveals how the spectral elements of a piece activate diverse registers and their specific color values, thereby creating tone color oppositions, combinations, and transformations of great power.

Low-Register Elements. In considering the spectrum photos and the analyses based upon them, one category of sounds requires special attention: those in the lowest registers (registers 0–3). For example, in the spectrum photo of the Tibetan Tantric chant "Invocation of Mahakala" (Photo 2), the sustained fundamental in the low men's voices, B^1, hardly ever appears. Only in the last half does it put in a weak, discontinuous appearance. Low-register sounds, generally, seem underrepresented in spectrum photos.

In order to understand this, we must return to the harmonic spectrum presented earlier, following Figure 5. There we observed that the sense of C^3 (131 Hz) is conveyed in two different ways: by vibrations at 131 Hz, and by the repetition of 131—the constant distance separating upper partials. It seems paradoxical, yet it is true that the human ear will hear a C^3 (131 Hz) if given a set of upper partials constantly separated by 131 cycles, even if no fundamental vibrations at that speed are present. In such a case, only the upper partials will appear in the spectrum photo, while the inferred fundamental will be absent. An inferred fundamental is an aural phenomenon with no direct external physical traces.

This is not at all uncommon in the sonic world. On the contrary, it has been turned into a constructive principal in musical instrument and audio equipment construction. As a consequence, however, the lowest registers of spectrum photos reveal much less activity than might be expected. Low notes often make their presence felt, spectrally, an octave or more higher than the register of their fundamental. Precisely because of its relative rarity, low-register spectral presence is a striking sonic color, and its appearance will often be noted in the commentaries.

Detail Photos. In Figure 5 we saw a detail photo—one that shows sonic cross-sections at specific isolated moments in time, each cross-section separated from its temporal and sonic context. Although this is not the preferred way of presenting spectra for our purposes here, there are instances in which it proves very useful. The details show all of the partials, or other spectral elements, sounding at a chosen moment, picturing each element as a spike (or peak). At the same time, the details show, by the height of each spike, the relative intensity of each spectral element. This adds another level to the information available through spectrum analysis.[10] In the details, the tuning of each spectral element is indicated via juxtaposition with a piano keyboard (at the lower edge of the details). The display of the details is even more sensitive to faint spectral traces than is that of the real-time spectrum photos, so that otherwise unobservable trace elements are sometimes visible.

Analytic Instrumentation and Limits. Ever since Helmholtz built resonators to separate and measure spectral elements, analysts of sound have developed increasingly sophisticated instruments for spectral analysis and for the display of sonic elements. Of these two important factors—display and analysis—it is more important, for our purposes, to speak of the former. (See Appendix A for a fuller discussion of analytic instruments.)

There are two common ways to display and transmit spectral information: numerical and graphic. Numerically, the display consists of a virtually endless tabulation of frequencies, intensities, and durations. Such a tabulation may have significant technical uses. For example, with it one could resynthesize a sonic context, or some semblance of it, after it has been analyzed. Still, this would be useful only to those few who are interested in reading a numerical tabulation for such technical purposes.

During the 1940s at Bell Laboratories and elsewhere, researchers developed ways of graphically representing the spectra of speech sounds. The book *Visible Speech* was a landmark in this field, illustrating spectra not only of single vowels and consonants but also of short words and phrases.[11] Such spectral modeling of auditory space and time is directly comparable to actual experience of those sonic features. The graphs also make it possible to portray great amounts of information changing rapidly over time and enable one to assimilate this information instantly. This is especially important for the analysis of musical works, whose duration and information content are much greater than those of brief verbal phrases. For these reasons, graphs are a particularly desirable medium for displaying the spectral formation of musical contexts and works. Austrian writer Hermann Broch has said of music that "it transmutes time into space."[12] The spectrum photos here reveal that process: they transmute time and its musical spectral formations into visible space: they make visible what was initially invisible. The seminal American musicologist Charles Seeger, in his melographs, made an early attempt to do this in the 1930s.

The principal point to understand here is that the spectrum photos are the result of an accumulation of human choices in the design and use of analytic and display instrumentation. Since the photos presented to the reader are the culmination of a chain of displays (the original cathode-ray tube display having been first photographed and then reproduced), there inevitably has been some loss of detail and gradation. Faint details and subtle gradations of gray and black have disappeared. Still, compared to the valuable information the photos reveal, what is lost is slight.

Even more important than technical limitations are the choices that have been made in performing and photographing the analyses—for example, the choice of time scale for the display of a given musical work. The scale can be slowed down so that the most fleeting sonic events appear in great detail: the sound of hammer striking string in a piano attack, say; or, in language, brief consonants and transients. The time scale can also be accelerated, so that an entire musical phrase appears summed up as a single visual instant. Both sorts of time scales have their advantages and disadvantages. With the slowest possible scale, even the shortest musical work would generate a virtually infinite amount of information, making it extremely difficult to assess the resulting mass of sonic detail. With the fastest scale, almost all details disappear; the display becomes difficult to follow, and specific sonic entities cannot be evaluated in terms of their surrounding context. Consequently, the time scale chosen for each spectrum photo lies between the two extremes. In any given case, it aims at displaying the body of individual events (notes, syllables, and so forth), as well as the musical whole (complete work, or substantial segment of one) to which they contribute. This makes it possible for us, as readers and analysts, to observe the interdependence of spectral details and the structures they create.

In the domain of loudness there is a similar choice. It is possible to display spectral elements that are virtually inaudible to humans; but with such a degree of magnification sounds that are hardly heard, and that bear no shaping significance, assume a prominence equal to that of important sounds. Indeed, since these photos are made from recordings, as the display approaches the limits of audibility it begins to show not the music but the sounds of the recording process.

Why have recordings been used for these analyses? Since the aim has been to discover the role of spectra in shaped musical structures, it is of crucial importance to begin with music (both composition and performance) that is a shaped structure. We need not just anybody singing "Strange Fruit" but Billie Holiday singing it, in order to discover the shaping forces in a performance of that power. The same is true of Schnabel performing Beethoven's Piano Sonata Opus 109. Such performances exist only as recordings and are accessible to readers in no other form. So the use of recordings seemed inevitable.

My associates and I devoted considerable time to comparing voices and instruments live and recorded, and in so doing discovered a fascinating and essential characteristic of musical performances: in the spectral shaping of a piece, the differences between two performers are often far greater and of far greater significance than those between live and recorded performances per se. Every time a pianist or conductor balances a sonority anew, every time a singer inflects a vowel differently, a new spectral nuance results, whether in live or recorded performance. Even in recordings made in the 1930s, particular performers produce striking results at unexpected extremes of the spectrum—results that present-day performers do not necessarily achieve in today's improved recordings or in live performance. All of this places a great deal of popular technological mythology in a new perspective.

The Analytic Background. Helmholtz directed the attention of scientists, linguists, and musicians to the role of spectra in creating the particular qualities of language and musical sounds, giving crucial impetus to sonic analysis in both domains. Thereafter, the evolution of theory and technology in the field accelerated, and significant, rapid technical developments—especially among the various types of electronic technology, such as sound recording—have become widespread.

The study of language sounds has made immense strides, primarily because of advances in phonology and phonetics, and has had repercussions extending into many other areas. Telephone, radio, sound recording—all the technologies of sonic transmission that have so changed our daily life—have depended upon and, in turn, stimulated the analysis of language sounds. Voice synthesis (speaking machines) and speech-responsive technology are among the most recent applications of sound spectrum research.

The analysis of musical sounds has been the stepchild of this development. Many sonic researchers since Helmholtz have been fascinated by musical sound—hardly able to keep away from the subject, even when it was not directly relevant to their scientific, technical, or commercial preoccupations. An example is Harvey Fletcher, who, as research director of Bell Laboratories from the 1930s to the 1950s, made landmark studies of the spectral formations of voice, keyboard, and stringed-instrument sounds.[13] Other studies of musical sound were carried out by researchers in Europe, India, and Japan. Such work prepared the way for the sonic analysis of entire, complex musical contexts.

Developed in the 1950s, electronic music synthesis using tape recording, sound synthesizers, and computers has become a boon to research. Since a precondition for successful sonic creation is an understanding of the nature and resources of the sonic medium, such electronic synthesis, where every sound is, or can be, specifically constructed, has created a need for sonic analysis and understanding. Moreover, sound synthesizers and computers have greatly expanded the sonic resources available for composition and research. For the first time in history, there exist instruments that can approximate the entire range of humanly audible sounds, permitting experimentation throughout this range.

As a consequence of these various streams of evolution, we are heirs to a new and enlarged understanding of the sounds of language and music. Using what we now know about sounds and the way in which they derive their qualities from spectral elements, linguistics has discovered the characteristic relationships and shapes of its constituent units—distinctive features, phonemes, syllables, and words—and has also identified some of the sonic structural principles of human language in general.

In contrast, musical analysis has as yet only ventured some first, hesitant steps. In the 1970s Pozzi Escot and I showed that by combining spectral data from individual instruments—data gathered by Harvey Fletcher and others—analyses of whole musical contexts and works could be carried out, even without a technology specifically available for that purpose.[14] Our work represented only one of the first systematic explorations of the idea of music as shaped, ordered spectral sonic contexts. Today, using the technology of spectral analysis and display, it is much easier to gather the spectral information and to obtain a view of the sonic elements themselves.

It is important, however, to avoid too mechanical a view of these evolutionary developments. The creative compositional imagination, and sometimes also the searching theoretical imagination, have often led the way into the world of sonic possibilities and understanding. Throughout the analyses presented here, one can see the musical imagination reaching out to touch and transform the world of sound. Think of the composer Varèse prompting and, with his sonic vision, challenging his friend Fletcher, the sonic researcher: "I dream of instruments obedient to my thought . . . with their contribution of a whole new world of unsuspected sounds."[15]

How will the rich and varied traditions of musical analysis interact with the new ideas that have resulted from technical progress? This book cannot provide a complete answer to this critical question, for the issues are as fundamental and far-reaching as they are novel. Still, a few preliminary observations are possible.

During the 1920s and 1930s the Austrian theorist Heinrich Schenker developed an analytical view of European music that has challenged and shaped the thinking of many musicians. Schenker conceived of music as flows of motion governed by the relationships of what he called the "chord of nature"—the major (and, to a lesser extent, minor) triads that he saw as deriving from the overtone series.[16] The spectrum photos presented here shed new light on this theory.

Among their most salient characteristics, for example, are vividly etched flows of spectral elements, these flows often providing a principal means of structuring the mass of sonic details. Sometimes, as Schenker correctly observed, these flows stretch over long spans of a musical work, during which they might be interrupted and resumed several times, and in which important elements might be foreshadowed or echoed. To this extent, the photos substantiate what might otherwise seem arbitrary theoretical fantasy.

At the same time, spectral analysis reveals the incredible variety of sonic morphologies. In the face of such diversity, Schenker's concept of a single reigning chord of nature seems no more than an idealistic simplification. Indeed, all of these spectral morphologies are chords of music's nature—from the harmonic spectral strands of a spoken vowel or an orchestra's single note, to the spectral noise bands of a spoken consonant or a bass drum's single stroke. There is an intimate connection between the diversity of available sonic morphologies and the diversity of global music cultures. The one sinister aspect of Schenker's theory—its denigration, on supposed theoretical and scientific grounds, of most of the world's music except that of eighteenth- and nineteenth-century Germanic culture—finds not the slightest support in spectrum analyses.[17]

Science, Technology, and Art. Some readers may wonder why this book, which focuses on the structural and expressive shaping of works of musical art, uses technology and concepts drawn from the physical and linguistic sciences. Can such a marriage of scientific and artistic analysis be legitimate and useful, either for science or for art?

Some scientists, artists, and laymen still subscribe to an outmoded Cartesian-Newtonian physical determinism, positing a dualistic universe in which humans stand forever outside the active physical forces, or are reduced to them. In their view, it is the physical forces that are real. However, advances in fields such as quantum physics—where the human observer directly affects the physical situation and the outcome of any investigations of it (and, furthermore, cannot be removed from it)—have shown that human considerations are part and parcel even of "physical" science. Humans affect, interpret, map, and model—in actions, images, sounds, verbal languages, or that special language we call mathematics—the universe and all of its processes and features. Our maps and models are our means of understanding the universe and its elements. Musical and artistic works are precisely such models; and, in a continuing process, we model these works in order to understand them as well.

If human participation is a factor in physical science, it can hardly be less so in the "human" sciences. Claude Lévi-Strauss stated that "theoretical knowledge is not incompatible with sentiment—knowledge can be both objective and subjective at the same time."[18] Possibly, indeed, knowledge *must* be so. This view is presented here not as dogma but rather as a basic premise underlying the book, in which technology and theory serve to illuminate the shape, structure, and power of diverse musics and in which, conversely, these qualities of the musics justify the technology and theory. Contrary to those who favor one or the other extreme—a wholly objective, nonhuman scientism or a wholly subjective, unscientific aestheticism—this study shows the domains of science and art to be profoundly related and richly interdependent.

The most ample precedent for the kind of analysis proposed here is to be found in the visual arts. From the beginning of the nineteenth century, the exploration of light and color engaged prominent scientists and artists: the physicists Clerk Maxwell, Thomas Young, and Helmholtz; the painters Turner, Delacroix, Monet, Pissarro, Seurat, and their many associates. Impressionism and Neo-Impressionism derive, primarily, from these artists' novel understanding and rendering of light and color. Goethe, to take another example, worked throughout his life on his *Farbenlehre* (Theory of Color), a book that Beethoven admired and Webern revered.[19] Its influence was widespread: Turner painted a major late canvas entitled *Light and Color: Goethe's Theory*. At the beginning of the nineteenth century neither a scientific nor an artistic theory of visual color existed. Artistically, color was widely held to be a domain that was intellectually incomprehensible, ruled only by taste.[20] By the end of the century, many of the basic principles of light and color were widely understood: a revolution in scientific and artistic theory and practice had taken place.

The impact of this revolution on artists is poignantly documented in many letters written in the 1880s by Vincent Van Gogh:

The *laws* of color are unutterably beautiful, just because they are *not accidental.*

. . . the study of color. I am always in hope of making a discovery there, to express the love of two lovers by a marriage of two complementary colors, their mingling and their opposition.[21]

In the twentieth century a continuation of the same revolution has led to artists as important as Henri Matisse, Josef Albers, and Mark Rothko, and to influential theories of color analysis developed by Johannes Itten at the Bauhaus, Arthur Pope at Harvard, and Albers at Yale.[22]

The camera has played an important role in this development, illustrating how technology can mediate between science and art: it is not widely realized that the first color photos were taken as early as 1856. Still photography, electric light, cinema, color television, and lasers have provided a technological workshop for color experimentation and discovery, just as recording, synthesizers, and computers have done for research in sound.

Studies of light and color are not the only aspects of visual art that reflect the influence of science and technology. The rationalization of artistic space through perspective was greatly solidified by Descartes's rationalization of geometric space in the seventeenth century, as well as by experiments with the *camera oscura,* the early predecessor of the camera. For sixteenth- and seventeenth-century artists, the *camera oscura* provided an exact analytic model of the perspective relationships of a scene. Vermeer was one of a number of Dutch and Italian artists who used *camera oscura* images as a basis for their paintings.[23]

The vivid color of a Turner painting and the realistic pictorial space of a Vermeer are thus not the result of pure aestheticism: they represent the union of artistic sensitivity with the insights and discoveries of science and technology. It is in the same unifying spirit, with the hope of attaining a comparable understanding of the sonic medium, that this book has been written. Its aim is not to celebrate technology and analytic theory in themselves, but rather to use these as means by which we can more deeply—more thoroughly—touch music's sound, and be touched by it.

Part I
Images of Sonic Structure

The primeval essence of color is a phantasmagorical resonance: light become music.

—JOHANNES ITTEN,
The Art of Color

1.
Voices

MUSIC FOR VOICE is one of the most potent of all human creative realms. Virtually every culture and epoch has fashioned one or more distinctive vocal images. Vocal music rivals spoken language in its quantity, ubiquity, and variety.

The examples of vocal music chosen for the first four spectrum photos suggest the range of this art. Roman Catholic Gregorian chant (Photo 1) and Tibetan Tantric chant (Photo 2) each embody centuries of sacred vocal traditions. Sonically, however, they are so different—one an evenly undulating melodic-linguistic stream; the other an unworldly sliding drone, deep, multiplex, and mysterious—that it is hard to believe they originate in the same human instrument. The improvisation of Billie Holiday (Photo 3) is, in contrast, the creative act of a single moment; but it, too, draws on diverse traditions of vocal song—primarily European and African, the two brought to intense focus at the moment of improvisation. Finally, Gyorgy Ligeti's *Lux Aeterna* (Photo 4) illustrates the work of a composer who is fully aware of recent linguistic and acoustic discoveries, these brought to a focus not in the act of improvisation but in the act of composition.

Vocal music weds musical sound to language sound. But although music has often been analyzed in itself, and although phonetics and phonology have been the subject of much research during the past eight decades, these studies have hardly ever been directly related. Spectrum photos now make this possible. They reveal that language sounds and musical features are collaborators of equal importance in creating the uniquely expressive sound shapes of vocal compositions.

PHOTO 1
GREGORIAN CHANT: "QUI SEDES, DOMINE"
Performed by monks from the Benedictine Abbey of Encalcat, Carcassonne, France
Duration: 2 minutes 25 seconds

Qui sedes, Domine, super Cherubim,	Lord, who dwell among the cherubim,
excita potentiam tuam, et veni.	stir up Thy strength and come.
Qui regis Israel, intende:	O ruler of Israel, shine forth,
qui deducis velut ovem Joseph.	You who lead Joseph like a flock.

Photo 1, illustrating a medieval Christian chant, gives us an immediate glimpse of the complex spectra generated by words and melody in a unison chorus of unaccompanied men's voices.

Photo 1. Gregorian chant, "Qui sedes, Domine."

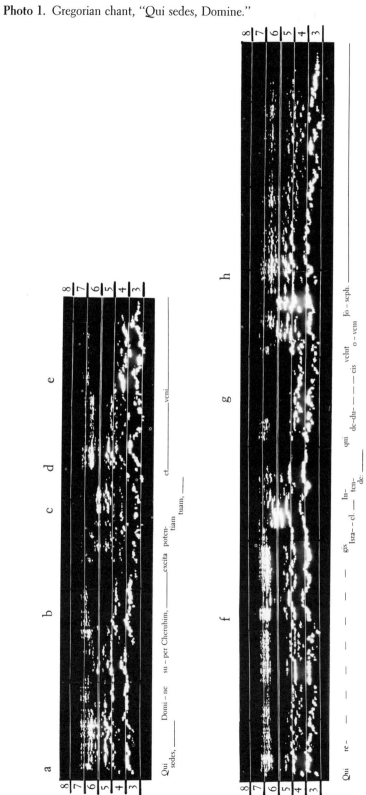

Fig. 6. "Qui sedes, Domine," beginning.

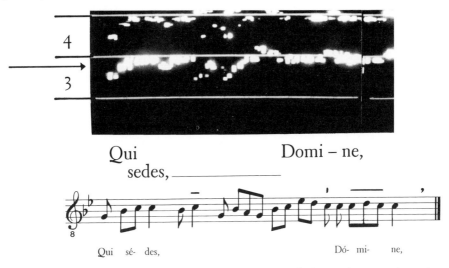

Qui
sedes,

Domi – ne,

Qui   sé- des,   Dó- mi-   ne,

The chant's melodic line (see Figures 6 and 7) can be traced in the lowest spectral strands of the photo. It begins by rising from registers 3 to 4 and later descends through all of register 3. Above the spectral tracings of the melody in Photo 1 are other tracings—upper partials, or overtones—which vary in quantity and density and which are produced by the combination of words, melody, and men's voices. In Figure 4 we saw how the spectral configuration changes at different moments of the chant, depending on the vowel being sung. We will now examine the shaping and sonic consequences of this spectral variety.

One of the first revelations of Photo 1 is that a single vowel, [ɛ] (eh), and its characteristic spectrum dominate the entire chant. Its unknown composer has chosen to dwell on this vowel at the beginning and end of each sentence of the text (lines 1 and 2 of the photo). The first prolonged word, "sedes" [sɛdɛs], immediately reiterates the [ɛ] spectrum, whose widely spread elements activate all the registers between the extremes of 3 and 7. The [ɛ] spectrum is also prolonged in line 1 in the words "Cherubim" and, especially, "et." In line 2 the words "regis" at the beginning and "Joseph" at the end show the same prolongation. Approximately 40 percent of the vowels of the text are [ɛ], and in terms of singing time the proportion is even greater— more than 60 percent. By stressing [ɛ] throughout, especially in the strategic framing positions at the beginning and end of each line, the composer has made this spectrum the most prominent thread in the chant's sonic fabric.

In sonic analysis each vowel reveals a characteristic spectrum. Even in speech, individual vowels are distinguished—and identifiable—by specific registral regions of intense resonance, known as *formants*. (The formants for four spoken vowels, which play an important role in "Qui sedes, Domine," are indicated by the peaks in Figure 5.) For the vowel [ɛ] the formant regions are in registers 5 and 6, reaching up toward register 7 (from about 700 to

Fig. 7. "Qui sedes, Domine."

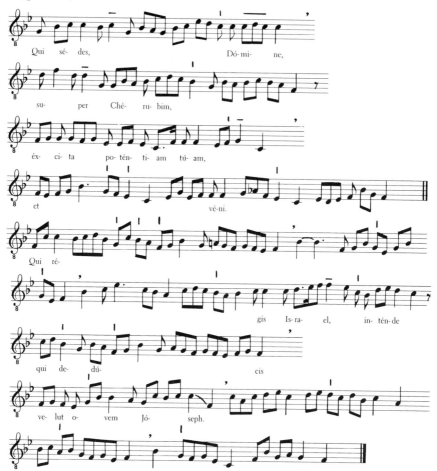

Qui sé- des, Dó- mi- ne,

su- per Ché- ru- bim,

éx- ci- ta po- tén- ti- am tú- am,

et vé-ni.

Qui ré-

gis Is- ra- el, in- tén- de

qui de- dú- cis

ve- lut o- vem Jó- seph.

1,800 Hz). These formant resonances, creating many strands of spectral activity over a wide range, are visible everywhere that [ɛ] occurs in Photo 1.

As the chant unfolds, however, the sonic character undergoes systematic transformation. Alternating with the recurrent prolongations of [ɛ] are a series of other brief passages, each of which is dominated by the prolongation of a different vowel. In order of appearance they are:

[i] "Cherub*i*m" and "ven*i*" in line 1
[a] "potenti*a*m tu*a*m" in line 1
[u] "ded*u*cis" in line 2.

What is especially striking about this progression of vowels is the way it successively eliminates the highest registers of spectral presence. Compared to the predominant [ɛ], which serves as a basis for sonic comparison, each of the later vowels eliminates one or more of the highest spectral registers:

[i] forms two isolated, widely spaced spectral strands, the lower and the stronger one in register 4, the higher, thinner, and weaker one around C^7; *most areas of registers 5 and 6 are mute.*

[a] concentrates its spectral elements around C^6 (1,000 Hz), at the border between registers 5 and 6; *higher elements in registers 6 and 7 are entirely absent.*

[u] concentrates its spectral elements around 400 Hz in register 4; *all higher regions in registers 5, 6, and 7 have been eliminated.*

Figure 4 shows clearly these vowel spectrum transformations—the vivid reduction in the highest spectral elements as the chant progresses from prolongations of [ɛ] and [i] to prolongations of [a] and [u]. Photo 1 presents these same moments in their complete spectral context.

So against the complex, high, ringing spectral resonances of the predominant [ɛ], there is a series of prolonged vowels that successively withdraws the high ringing resonances and concentrates the spectral elements in the lower, darker registers. This spectral withdrawal and shift of registral focus creates, in the middle of lines 1 and 2 on the words "tuam" and "deducis," particularly suave, mellow sonorities. With their prolonged [a] and [u] spectra, these sonorities contrast poignantly with the overriding [ɛ] to which the chant always returns. One could regard each vowel as a particular sonic theme in an unfolding play of ever more contrasting sonic themes.

Many people—even some musicians—think that when music is added to words, it is the music that gives shape and expression to the words. Here we see that this is only a half-truth: in "Qui sedes, Domine" the words, especially their vowels, *orchestrate* the music, giving each melodic note (the notated fundamental pitch) a specific array of resonating spectral elements (the vowel formants). Depending upon the vowel, these spectral resonances can be relatively low, grave, and dark; or high, acute, and bright. In contrast to the bright referential [ɛ] there is a succession of darkening vowels, culminating, in the word "deducis," in the most intense opposition: between the monolithic, grave [u] and the complex, acute [ɛ]. The sonic effect is similar to that produced when a French horn takes over a melody from a trumpet; or, to use another analogy, when one modulates an audio system in the course of the melody so that the treble is weakened and the bass augmented—the audio system in this case being a chorus of men's voices in its cathedral setting. This powerful, evolving sonic contrast results from the way in which the composer has chosen to prolong certain vowels.

In addition, the composer has chosen a melodic contour that reflects the vowel oppositions. The melodic range of the chant is unusually wide—a biregistral span of almost one and a half octaves, compared to the more usual one-octave limitation of chant melodies. In the areas of the predominant [ɛ] vowel, the melody ascends to its linear peaks in register 4, on the words "sedes," "regis," "Israel" (the principal linear apex of the chant), "intende," and "Joseph" (see Figure 8). On the other hand, where the vowels darken to

Fig. 8. "Qui sedes, Domine," excerpt.

(ré-)   gis Is- ra- el,   in- ten- de

Fig. 9. "Qui sedes, Domine," excerpt.

éx- ci- ta   po- tén- ti- am   tú- am,

[a] and [u], the line descends to its linear depths at the bottom of register 3, especially in the phrases "excita potentiam tuam" and "deducis velut ovem Joseph" (which add to the repetition of [a] and [u] an almost equally dark repeated [o]—see Figure 9).

The chant's linear extremities, high and low, exactly reflect its opposition of acute and grave vowel spectra. As the melodic line rides up to its peaks, the vowel [ɛ] and its acute spectral elements appear as well. As the melodic line descends to its depths, the brightest spectral resonances are withdrawn, and the vocal sonorities turn dark and dull, with the vowels [a], [o], and [u]. The structure of the chant replicates the same opposition in two different ways: at the micro, linear level and at the macro, spectral level. The coordination of these transformations, linear and spectral, creates the special structural force and expressive power of this chant. The two complementary structural levels consistently magnify each other.

Analysts of Gregorian chant have heretofore confronted many mysteries which, more often than not, have resisted analysis. The subtle shadings and colorings of chant have been particularly elusive. It is in some ways surprising that the analysis of chant sonority—the linkage of its verbal colors to its melodic motions—leads to a new understanding of its contrasts, transformations, and shaping. Yet because this music is so rooted in words and their expression, it seems natural, too, that the pairing of its verbal and musical sounds should help unlock its structural and expressive mysteries.[1]

PHOTO 2
TIBETAN TANTRIC CHANT: INVOCATION OF MAHAKALA
Performed by eleven monks from Gyuto Monastery, Lhasa, Tibet
Duration: 4 minutes 13 seconds

By the power of the Lama, his root lineage, the three Jewels and work of the Buddha,

By the force of my secret teachings, mantra, meditation, and mudra,

And by the assemblage of suitable sacred offerings both inner and outer

Having pure true dharmakaya (self-nature),

Filling the earth, the heavens, and the vastness of space,
May there appear before my eyes in fulfillment of my vow
The Wisdom Mahakala with his retinue,
Giving bliss untainted, fulfilling all aspirations.[2]

At several leading Tibetan monasteries, Gyuto and Gyume in particular, monks have cultivated for centuries one of the most astonishing sonic contexts in all world music. To begin with, the monks sing in an ultra-bass register rarely reached by human voices. Moreover, each singer produces more than one note at a time: "Each of the voices chanting produces simultaneously a monotone fundamental and a harmonic overtone that rings out with great clarity, such that every monk is singing a two-note chord."[3]

Each voice brings the spectral elements forward to the listeners' immediate perception. Spectral elements do not merely color a single fundamental pitch; they become active participants in the sonic foreground. At least one sonic analyst, Kenneth Stevens, has begun the documentation of this remarkable vocal technique.[4] Still, the *musical structure* of such a music as the Invocation of Mahakala—with its sliding ultra-bass voices and their haunting audible spectra, set against ringing cymbals and isolated, ominous bass-drum beats—has, as far as I know, never been studied.

Tibetan vocal technique makes available not merely a single distinctive sound, but a whole set of vocal transformations. In Tibet the vocal nuances are inscribed in a unique graphic notation and carefully rehearsed for performance. Photo 2 reveals the role of these sonorities in creating the musical structure of the Invocation.

We first notice a sustained voice spectrum that recurs throughout lines 1 (starting at b) and 2. Its principal partials emphasize two different notes, B and $D^\#$:

B^4, 496 Hz (Partial 8) $D^{\#5}$, 620 Hz (Partial 10)
B^3, 248 Hz (Partial 4) $D^{\#4}$, 310 Hz (Partial 5)
B^2, 124 Hz (Partial 2)

(These emphasized notes and partials can also be seen in Detail b.)

It is the spectrum's balanced emphasis of B and $D^\#$ that conveys the sense that each voice is singing two notes at once. While the fundamental, B^1 (62 Hz), bears virtually no vibrational energy, these five partials strongly replicate the two opposing notes, B and $D^\#$, in several registers. The opposition is not only of distinct notes, but also of distinct registral colors: B's sound in register 4 and lower, $D^\#$'s in register 4 and higher. Each note brings into focus both its specific pitch class and a specific spatial-registral coloration. The deep, grave B is evoked down to B^1, while the mysterious spectral $D^\#$ floats clearly out of the more acute registers, 4 and 5, above. The opposition of notes and the opposition of registral colors reinforce each other.

Although this fascinating, complex sonority dominates the voice part of line 1, it is hardly the only vivid sonority in the piece. Line 1 is full of addi-

Photo 2. Tibetan Tantric chant, Invocation of Mahakala.

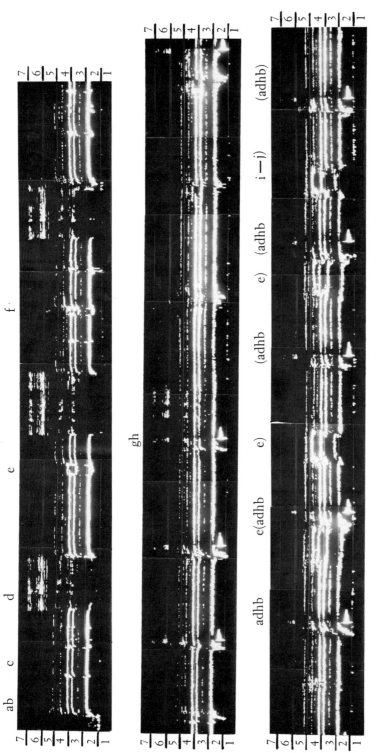

Photo 2, Details. Voices, *b*, *e*, *j*, and *i*; cymbals, *d* and *g*; bass drum, *h*.

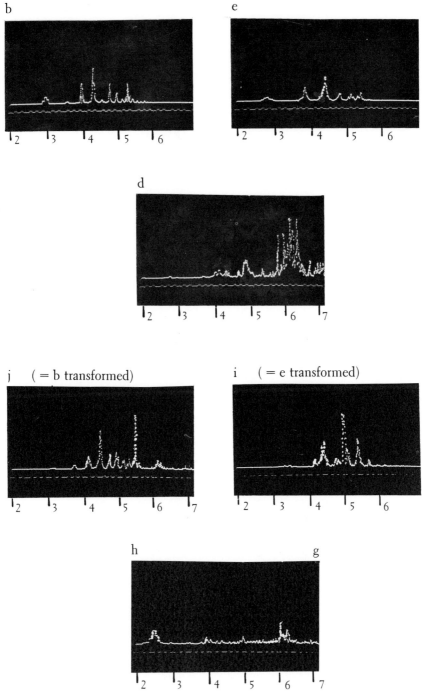

b

e

d

j   (= b transformed)

i   (= e transformed)

h   g

tional vocal nuances, each of which turns out to bear thematic significance in the Invocation's later play of contrasting sonic qualities. We have already observed in a single sonority the oppositions of pitches, B and D$^\sharp$, and of registral colors, grave and acute. To these line 1 adds: opposition of sliding, oblique motion to level stasis (see a/b in the photo); opposition of consonant, percussive attack to vowel-like, sustained resonance (see c/b); and opposition of dense, complex sonorities to sparse, hollow ones (see b/e). These paired sonic contrasts become magnified as the piece continues.

There are, for example, the vocal slides that begin the piece and that also begin every subsequent vocal phrase (a in Photo 2). The slides always lead into the dominating vocal sonority (b). Each of these repeated gestures opposes an oblique sliding entrance to the level stasis of the sustained dominating vocal complex. In line 2 these rising sliding entrances are much intensified, appearing as wider, more frequent, and more rapid ascents. Then, toward the middle of line 2 (after g-h) and throughout line 3, the complex dominating spectrum itself executes a number of prolonged sliding motions, so that the initial spectral complex (or more complex variants of it) is built on other fundamentals than the original B^1—for example, upon C$^{\sharp 2}$ at j, as is shown in Detail j.

The opposition of oblique sliding motion to level stasis found in the very first gesture comes to characterize the structure of the Invocation as a whole. The predominantly level line 1, with its triple textual invocations—"By the power . . . By the force . . . And by the assemblage . . ."—stands opposed to the ever-increasing oblique sliding throughout the remainder of the music, with its envisioned appearance of the Wisdom Mahakala.

The next pair of opposing sonic qualities may be even more important, for it leads us to consider the interplay between the men's chorus and the odd percussion battery—cymbals and ultra-bass drum—that accompanies it. Note the spectral *knots* that briefly interrupt the otherwise continuous vocal sound of the first phrase (at c in Photo 2). These are consonants, whose attacks momentarily break into and thicken the spectral strands of the choral vowels. These knots add a new sonic contrast—consonant attacks opposed to sustained vowels—that will be enhanced by the percussion instruments. It is apparent early in the piece that the percussion instruments do not merely contrast with the voices; rather, they magnify one (and in fact several) of the oppositions already presented by the voices alone.

Throughout line 1 the sustained ultra-bass voice spectrum alternates with punctuating cymbal clashes played by the choral leader. Like the voices, the cymbals present a flow of distinctive attack articulations followed by sustained resonances: quasi-consonants followed by quasi-vowels. The cymbal technique employed—a horizontally held cymbal is struck at its edge by a vertically held one—allows the choral leader to mimic the variety of plosives (p, b, t, d) and fricatives (f, v, s, z) in spoken and sung language. A cymbal attack is followed either by other articulations (as in accelerating rhythmic patterns) or by ringing resonance, just as choral consonants are followed by sustained vowels. In this way the cymbals reenact the opposition between consonant attacks and resonating sustained vowels of the men's voices.

The spectra of the cymbals and voices show, under close scrutiny, an uncanny point of similarity: the lowest band of cymbal resonance (between B^3 and $D^{\#4}$) *coincides exactly* with the strongest and closest of the principal partials in the voices' predominating sonority (compare *b* and *d* in Photo 2, and Details *b* and *d*). The cymbals and voices "speak" in the same narrow region at the intersection of registers 3 and 4. But their spectral resonances radiate from that shared center over vast opposing regions of musical space—as distant as registers 1 and 7.

Consequently, the voice/cymbal alternations in line 1 reenact the initial grave/acute opposition of the voices alone on a vast scale—throughout the piece's entire range. The voices (covering registers 1–5) are themselves opposed, as grave, to the cymbals' acute (covering registers 3–7). This larger opposition resonates over seven separate registers of musical space.

It must be recognized, too, that the cymbals on their own present yet another variant of this same registral opposition. For it is the cymbals' articulative attacks that speak spectrally in registers 3 and 4 (grave), whereas it is their long, complex, sustaining resonances that vibrate over wide regions of registers 4–7 (acute, see *d* in the photo).

At first, no two media seem more different and less compatible than men's voices and cymbals. But the spectral elements of the Invocation reveal their shared, as well as their dramatically opposing, sonic features. Growling, resonating male voices and clanging, ringing cymbals: both alternate abrupt attacks with long complex resonances, which they emit in spectral strands and bands from a shared sonic center toward the most remote, opposing limits of auditory space.

In the Tibetan Tantric tradition, voices do not so much present a text as evoke and camouflage it. Nonsense syllables and syllabic sonic variants are both mixed in with the actual text.[5] The result is a flow of distinctive vocal articulations and resonances in which the sacred textual details are hidden from the uninitiated, even while its deepest meanings are evoked. The cymbals may be thought of as carrying to the farthest extreme the abstract, stylized, and varied presentation of the opposing sonic features of the text. A particularly striking moment occurs in line 2, *gh*. It is the only place in the Invocation where voices and cymbals resonate continuously together, joined by an ultra-deep bass drum (*h*), all vividly evoking the text: "Filling the earth, the heavens, and the vastness of space . . ."

There is yet another thematic sonic opposition in line 1: the opposition of sparse, hollow spectra to the prevailing dense, complex spectra. The dense prevailing vocal sonorities of line 1 are interrupted not only by the sliding ascents and consonant knots already observed, but also by a contrasting spectrum which radically thins out and centers the prevailing complex sound (see Figure 10). Tibetan vocal technique, with its high degree of spectral control, allows for a whole array of different spectral configurations. At *e* and *f* the rich

Fig. 10. Invocation of Mahakala, contrasting spectra: Photo 2, *b*, *e*, *f*, and Details *b* and *e*.

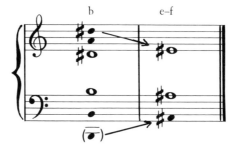

prevailing vocal sound, with its contrasting extremities, is momentarily eradicated through a striking spectral simplification. At those instants the sonic complexities seem to "come into focus," only to diffuse again immediately into the predominant vocal complex.

The structural climax of the Invocation occurs in line 3 of Photo 2, where, with ever-increasing speed and intensity, all the opposing thematic sounds and spectra whirl against each other (see Photo 2, the repeated sequence *adhbe*). As the elements recur in this accelerating juxtaposition, each is intensified. For example, the principal vocal sonority, *b*, becomes ever richer in spectral complexity. By the time it appears as *j*, its original six sounding partials have grown to eleven and its sound approximates the resonance of a throng in full cry (see Detail *j*). Furthermore, the men's voices are in almost constant oblique sliding fluctuation, rising and falling by minute intervals around their original locus, B.

In this climactic region of the Invocation, every high cymbal attack, as well, is instantly answered by a beat of the ultra-bass drum (elements *d* and *h*), repeatedly emphasizing the grave/acute opposition in an intense percussive form. And finally, the sparse, centered vocal sonority, *e*, interrupts every vocal phrase with greater emphasis and with heightened pitch intensity. At the final juxtaposition of opposing vocal spectra (*i* and *j*), the gap in pitch and spectral makeup between the two vocal sonorities, spectrally sparse and spectrally dense, has grown to astonishing proportions (see Figure 11). Having whirled its constituent sonic elements to this paroxysm of opposition, the Invocation, to conclude, slides back into nothingness (Photo 2, line 4).

The spectrum photo and details make it possible to define the array of vocal and percussive sonic oppositions and to observe how the quality of sonic contrast is built up to its final climactic intensity. The vocal sonorities turn out to be the source of an unusually evocative, powerful musical structure. The finest vocal nuances of pitch, spectrum, register, and attack generate a multitude of transformations and contrasts.

The Invocation, finally, can be understood as an icon of Tibetan Tantra itself, with its cosmic vision of bliss attained by intensifying every experience to its ultimate extremity.[6] Whether it is the opposition of voices to cymbals and drum, or (within the voice sounds themselves) of ultra-deep men's fun-

Fig. 11. Invocation of Mahakala, transformed spectra.

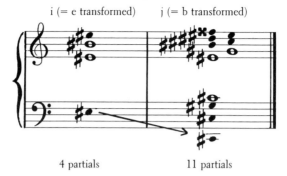

damentals to floating high spectral sounds, or of sliding to level sonorities, or of complex, thronging sounds to sparse, hollow ones—at every turn, each sonic character seems to confront its opposite extreme. How radically different this vision and the ensuing sonic structure are from the gradual, linear, step-by-step, contained transformations of the Gregorian chant.[7]

PHOTO 3
BILLIE HOLIDAY AND LEWIS ALLEN: "STRANGE FRUIT"
Performed by Billie Holiday, accompanied on piano
Duration: 2 minutes 25 seconds

Innumerable subtleties of vocal art emerge from a close look at this spectrum photo. It provides an especially appropriate notation for tracing the finely nuanced linkage of word and sound in Holiday's singing—a singing that in its creative essence transcends, or perhaps corrects, our usual sense of the word *performance*.

The first stanza (Photo 3, line 1) foreshadows, in microcosm, the whole song. Holiday's singing of the first word, "Southern," immediately brings into focus the performance's conjunction of sound and sense. Her improvised bending of its first syllable, "Sou-," is a thematic nuance that she recalls with every reappearance of the word or its root. This can be seen and heard at "the southern breeze," the climactic apex of line 1; and at "the gallant South," ironically beginning stanza 2, line 2—where the bend down to the lowest voice note, E^3, recalls the same bend at the beginning of line 1.

Photo 3 also shows, at the beginning of line 1, the infinitesimal silence by which Holiday separates the textually crucial word "Southern" from the following word, "trees."

Note bending is a motif that recurs with ever-increasing intensity. "The gallant South" is immediately echoed with growing irony at "sweet and fresh," again bending to the voice's lowest depth. Then a string of increasingly bent phrases—"of burning flesh," "for the crows to pluck," and "for the rain to gather"—leads with gathering intensity to the explicit recall of the first stanza at "for the wind to suck." The wavering undulations of the

Photo 3. Billie Holiday, "Strange Fruit."

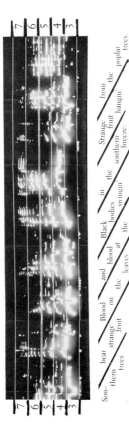

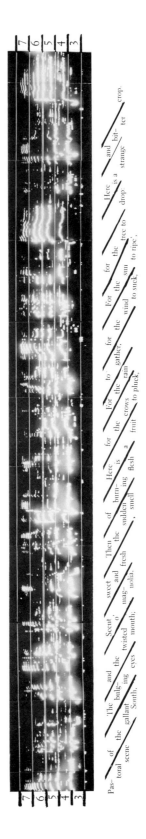

"southern breeze" in line 1 have become the agonizing bends of the sucking "wind" in line 2. Finally, the closing rhyme words of the song, "drop" and "crop," convey with an elaborately shaped sound sculpture the most prolonged and intricately bent contours of the entire song.

It is no longer news that the Afro-American vocal tradition, a tradition Holiday helped create, employs note bending as a principal expressive means. What may be news, however, is the variety of bent-note gestures Holiday has at her command, and the structural consistency and transformational scope of their employment. The descending arches bending to the vocal depths on "Southern," "gallant South," and "sweet and fresh" stand in clear contrast not only to their level, unbent neighbors, but also to the hovering breeze and wind-blown melodic shapes—their sounds reflecting the textual meaning—that are the dominating feature of all of the song's apical, climactic moments.

It may be surprising to discover in "Strange Fruit," just as in "Qui sedes, Domine" (Photo 1), that vowel spectra orchestrate these complex vocal contours with a design of diverse colors of changing vowels. In the first stanza, vowel colors are organized into a particularly stark opposition. The accumulating acute vowels of the climactic line—"Bl*a*ck bod*ie*s sw*i*ngin' *i*n the southern br*ee*ze"—contrast sharply with the grave vowels of the preceding lines, their gravity underscored by the repeated [u] of the first pair of rhyming words, "fr*u*it" and "*r*oot."

The spectral consequences of this opposition of vowels can be clearly seen in line 1 of Photo 3. During the first half of the line, the highest register, 7, is almost entirely mute. Then, at the center of line 1 the entire phrase "black bodies swingin' in the southern breeze" richly and continuously activates register 7. At the same time register 3, the lowest register, falls mute. As in the Gregorian chant, the spectral transformation from grave to acute is here underscored by a simultaneous melodic ascent to the linear apex, high in register 4. Indeed the climactic intensity of this phrase results from the concerted force of the heightened melodic activity rising to its linear apex, together with the sustained spectral acuity and the most prolonged bent-note shaping yet to occur in the performance. Each of these structural forces makes its independent contribution to the intensity of the phrase. They do so at the exact moment that the text explicitly presents its terrible generating image, "Black bodies swingin' . . . ."

Whereas the first stanza of the song directly presents its textual and sonic features, the second stanza (Photo 3, line 2) shows a far more complex interplay. We have already noticed how, by bending the voice to its depths, the phrases "the gallant South" and "sweet and fresh" are ironically undercut. As at the beginning of the first stanza, the opening of the second stanza largely locates the vocal melody in register 3, while its spectra omit register 7.

Just after the word "fresh," the melodic and spectral emphasis begins to change. Unlike that of the first stanza, this transformation is not immediate and direct. Rather, in the following phrases, especially with the words "burning," "crows," "wind," and "tree," the melodic line and the vowel spectra both flare upward, only to be repeatedly undercut. Once again prolonged words, especially "wind" and "tree," offer acute vowels that light up the highest spectral regions as they are prolonged.

Line 2 of Photo 3 shows this succession of spectral and linear peaks, the intensity of each one repeatedly undercut, only to rise again almost immediately. This growing intensity is finally and fully released with the savage concluding phrase: ". . . for the tree to drop: / Here is a strange and bitter crop." As at the climax of stanza 1, there appears a string of acute, stressed, and prolonged vowels (italicized). We find, in the last half of line 2, the only sustained activation since the climax of line 1 of acute vowels in register 7, and of melodic motion through the higher regions of register 4. The coordinated structural forces that forged the climax of stanza 1 all join again here to create and maintain the climactic ending of the entire piece. Together they complete the flowering of the oppositions that were presaged in the brief climax of line 1. They create a haunting ending that entirely fulfills the structural requirements established in the first stanza.

Holiday's singing displays one especially interesting technical feature. Despite the complex, subtly bent contours of her performance, the sung words are conveyed with clarity—indeed, with great force. This might seem paradoxical. Some analysts of the acoustics of singing have made much of a particular resonance common in the European bel canto vocal tradition.[8] This vocal resonance has been called the "singer's formant" and is located in the lower half of register 7. For the most part, Holiday's singing does not reveal any added spectral presence in that region. Spectral elements in the region appear principally with those vowels ([I] and [i]) whose ordinary formant resonance is strong there. Rather than overlaying, and potentially obscuring, other vowels with this added resonance, Holiday's vowel spectra are particularly speech-like. Indeed, we have already seen that the structure and intensity of the piece derive from the design and placement of these distinctive, unobscured vowel spectra.

It is only when they play a particular role in this larger structural scheme that Holiday's vowels are modified. Notice the way in which she colors "fresh" (in line 2) by suppressing its highest and brightest spectral elements in order to achieve its ironic darkening (compare with "flesh," line 2). An opposing instance can be observed at the very end of the performance, where each of the closing rhyme-words, "drop" and "crop," reveals spectral traces of the "singer's resonance" in register 7, a resonance not belonging to the spoken [a] vowel of these words. The added resonance serves perfectly to enhance the spectral intensity of register 7 that is a crucial feature of this climactic moment of the song. Holiday clearly possessed such resonance as one element of her vocal resources. Rather than applying it as a constant impasto over every sound, she shades and colors each vowel to fit the meaning and structure of the particular moment and situation. The spectral resonances are used to attain clear structural and expressive ends—they are combined with the other sonic possibilities of words and voices to be molded, as here, into a significant shape.[9]

PHOTO 4

GYORGY LIGETI: LUX AETERNA

Performed by the North German Radio Chorus, Hamburg: Helmut Franz, conductor

Duration: 8 minutes

Lux aeterna luceat eis,	Eternal light, illuminate them,
Domine, cum sanctis tuis	Lord, with Thy holiness
in aeternam, quia pius es.	forever, because Thou art forgiving.
Requiem aeternam dona eis,	Eternal rest grant them,
Domine, et lux perpetua luceat eis.	Lord, and with perpetual light illuminate them.

The text of *Lux Aeterna* is taken from the Requiem Mass; it is the point at which the ritual of death is permeated by a vision of eternal light. In Ligeti's imagination, the unending light spectrum has been translated into the uninterrupted sonic spectrum of a chorus of sixteen voices. The composer has described this continuously changing, unbroken sonic stream: "It is like a reflection on the surface of a pool that is slowly ruffled; and when it becomes smooth, a new reflection is visible."[10]

Photo 4 shows the gradual evolution of the piece over its eight-minute duration. The sonic form floods out from a single centered spectral strand, until it fills all of audible space with sound—and then just as gradually dissolves. The sixteen voices take up sounds from one another, adapting the technique of canonic imitation. To avoid breaking the sonic flow, the composer repeatedly specifies that consonants are *not* to be pronounced. Language is reconceived as an undisturbed stream of vowels and their subtly changing spectra. Unending light is interpreted as a variously shaded beam of continuous vocal sound, transcending the limits of human breath (a metaphor for human life) and the conventions of language.

The quality of sonority at any moment in the piece depends largely on which voices are singing—female or male, high or low—and on which vowels are being sung. The distribution of text among the various voices creates specific fields, or "pools" of sonority:

SENTENCE 1 (PHOTO 4, LINE 1)

a   "Lux"—women's voices, F^4 unison only

b   "aeterna"—all women's voices

c   "luceat eis"—high voices (women and tenors)

d   "Domine"—basses falsetto (alto register)

e   "cum sanctis tuis"—tenors

fg "in aeternam, quia pius es"—all men's voices

SENTENCE 2 (PHOTO 4, LINE 2)

h   "Requiem aeternam dona eis" and "quia pius es"—all voices

i   "Domine"—basses

jlm "et lux perpetua luceat eis"—low voices (altos and basses)

[*k* "luceat eis"—brief interpolations in high voices (sopranos and tenors)]

Photo 4. Gyorgy Ligeti, *Lux Aeterna.*

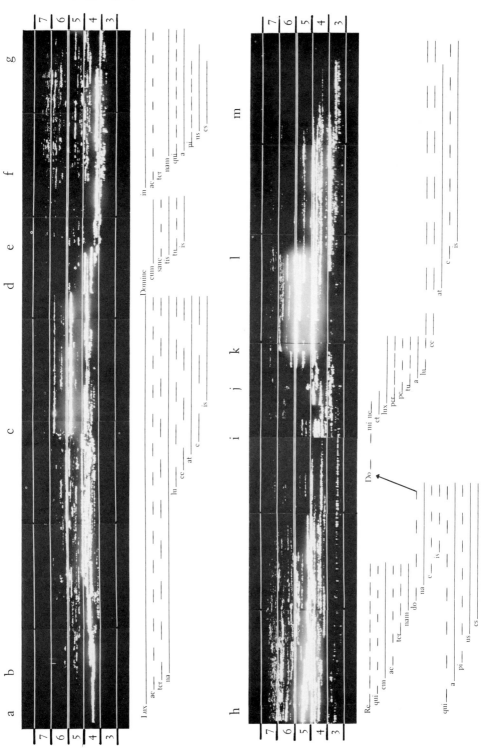

This distribution of text and voices organizes Sentences 1 and 2 into vivid sonic oppositions. The oppositions are especially apparent when we compare the beginnings of the two sentences:

SENTENCE 1, BEGINNING (a)	SENTENCE 2, BEGINNING (h)
Single pitch, F^4	A mass of simultaneous pitches, up to twelve at the same time
Single voice type, women's	All voice types—men's and women's, high and low
Single register, register 4	Fundamentals spread through all four registers of the piece (registers 2–5)
Single vowel, [u]	Multiple vowels, derived from the superposition of two lines of text
Single spectral element, the fundamental in register 4	The most complex and extended spectrum of the piece, stretching from register 2 to register 7

The sonic oppositions of these beginnings are characteristic of their sentences as a whole. Sentence 1 is consistently simpler in its sonorities and less directed to the extremities of spectral space than sentence 2. It displays a succession of single, discrete voice groups: women's (ab); high voices (women's and tenors, c); basses (d); tenors (e); men's voices (fg). Although it gradually opens out from its single beginning midpoint in space into an ever-wider space of fundamentals and spectra, its individual areas of activity and motion tend to be narrow. For example, its fundamentals are almost entirely located in registers 3 and 4, the central registers of the piece, and remain for long stretches in only one of these. Although it largely eschews the registral extremities, its general locus of activity is in the *higher* voices: women's voices and tenors play a leading role. The basses are heard alone only falsetto, in the alto register (register 4, at d). Photo 4, line 1, shows the sentence as it gradually widens and grows in spectral richness through the first four minutes of the piece.

Sentence 2, on the other hand, tends toward the multiplex, with consistent juxtaposition of the diverse and the extreme. It begins with the most complex mixture of notes, registers, voices, vowels, and spectral elements of the entire piece. As it unfolds and dissolves, it tends to isolate the extremities and to place them in direct oppositions. For example, the low basses' "Domine" (ij) is followed by the high sopranos' "luceat eis" (k); the latter is a luminous moment sonically, and can be seen as such in the photo. Indeed, the concluding statement of "luceat eis" (l) presents the only soundings in the piece of the extreme highest and lowest notes of the voices, B^5 and D^2, momentarily superimposed on each other.

Despite some instants of high-register presence, which are necessary to create these intense registral oppositions, the general locus of activity of sentence 2 is in the lower registers. For example, the long conclusion of the piece focuses canonically on the lowest registers of the lowest voices of each sex, altos and basses. Throughout the entire sentence there is a gradual disappearance of the highest spectral registers: registers 7, 6, and ultimately 5 (Photo 4, *i* and *lm*). In opposition to the ever-widening spectral formations of sentence 1, those of sentence 2 diminish and dissolve as they descend (compare Photo 4, lines 1 and 2).

The spectral design of the entire piece is realized with notable care and subtlety. The vivid opposition between the beginnings of the two lines parallels their contrasting vowel spectra. The beginning of sentence 1 insists exclusively on the lowest, dullest vowel spectrum, the [u] of "Lux." Indeed, the isolated beginning pitch, F^4, lies squarely in the formant area of that vowel (see Figure 5), so that the voice sound is totally concentrated in that single point of resonance (Photo 4, *a*). In contrast, at the beginning of sentence 2 the verbal superposition is arranged so that there is the constant presence of the vowel [i], whose wide, complex spectrum includes the highest vowel resonance (register 7):

$$\text{"Re } - \nearrow \text{qui} \searrow - \text{ em} \quad \text{(ae-)}$$
$$\text{"qui} \nearrow - \text{ a } - \searrow \text{pi}\text{—(us)}$$

Indeed, [i], with its widely split formant (registers 4 and 7; see Figure 5), offers a sonic model for the complex, wide-ranging total sonority that Ligeti provides for it at *h*. The emphasis of [i] at that point results directly from the composer's decision to overlap texts: retaining "quia *pius* es" from the end of sentence 1, while "Requiem aeternam" begins sentence 2.

In this way the [u] / [i] contrast of the sentence beginnings—with the centered, monolithic [u] spectrum opposed to the extremely widespread, multiplex, acute [i]—is magnified by Ligeti's distribution of text and music. As in musics as diverse as "Qui sedes, Domine" and "Strange Fruit," here too the principal structural contrast of the piece coincides with, and fully reflects, the sonic opposition provided by the textual vowels. Those vowels provide the spectral *orchestration*, an orchestration that plays an important role in creating the structural shape. In *Lux Aeterna* the two sonic forces, musical and verbal, combine to create at *h* the very summit of the compositional structure—the goal of the spectral unfolding of line 1, and the beginning of the sonic dissolution of line 2.

Photo 4 reveals many other instances of precise spectral design and opposition. In sentence 1, for example, the introduction of the words "luceat eis" (*c*, middle of line 1) is a remarkable sonic event. The soprano shift from register 4 up to A^5 at that moment provides the first, and only, sounding fundamental in that spatial region in all of line 1. However, Photo 4 reveals that the same region has already been activated for some time by *spectra* of the preceding word, "aeterna." Spectrally, register 5 has already been made resonant and alive. The soprano appearance of A^5 with the words "luceat eis" is not just a new event, but rather a confirmation and culmination of the pre-ceding spectral life. The spectral spirit has taken on vocal flesh.

A similar process at *g*, toward the end of line 1, prepares for the coming spectral peak at the beginning of the line 2—but with subtle differences. At the end of line 1 there is a momentary disappearance of high-register reso-nance (in registers 5 and 7, caused by the momentary removal of [i]). For this brief moment just prior to the spectral peak, the spectral resonance turns dull and grave. In this way the complexity and brightness of line 2's spectral peak at *h* is intensified by local contrast. At local levels as well as on the largest scale, the principal oppositions of the sonic design are reenacted.

Indeed, the growth of spectral complexity toward the end of line 1 re-quires some further observations. By setting there the words "in aeternam, quia pius es" (*fg*), the composer expands the sonic activity outward in two opposing directions. As the fundamentals of the men's voices *descend* from register 4 into register 3, the spectral regions activated by the repeated [e] and [i] vowels *ascend* into registers 6 and 7. The setting of this phrase, with its diverging fundamentals and spectra, prepares the listener for the full blos-soming of texture and spectrum at the beginning of line 2.

Having observed this diversity of choral voicings and spectral forma-tions, one can begin to understand the many colorations Ligeti evokes within *Lux Aeterna*'s continuous eight-minute sonic beam. In Photos 1–3, the de-gree to which the creator's sonic achievement may have been either conscious or intuitive was uncertain; with Ligeti, this relationship is perhaps easier to understand. Rainer Wehringer, writing about Ligeti's earlier tape composi-tion *Artikulation*, noted "Ligeti's detailed study of the literature on phonet-ics," where his special interests were "analyses of acoustic spectrum and proportion of noise in sounds."[11]

The sonic creation in *Lux Aeterna* is, at least in part, a result of con-scious knowledge. Spectrum photos offer one means of making that knowl-edge, and the resulting sonic design, manifest. We can see how Ligeti has given musical shape to the text, as well as how the text lends sonic shape to the music. In *Lux Aeterna* the two elements, text and music, coalesce to achieve Ligeti's stated compositional ideal of "a higher unifying complex."[12]

2.
Instruments

HUMAN VOICES and languages represent one repository of spectral formations and tone colors available to the musical imagination. Musical instruments represent the other. Nearly all cultures and epochs augment the resources and palette offered by the voice with those offered by musical instruments. The craftsmanship and technology of a particular culture or epoch are not only invoked but also highly refined in the production of the instruments that are the source of their music's spectral formations and tone colors. Energy, technical skill, and the utmost sensitivity continue to be devoted to this task; recent advances in the audio industry are merely the latest of many centuries' worth of efforts to use technology to create sources of musical sound.

The image of an instrumental repository, or storehouse, of spectral formations and sounds is useful up to a point. But we must beware of separating the evolution of musical instruments from the evolution of music: they are not two separate processes but one, dynamic and complex. While the musical imagination makes use of the available instrumental sounds of its cultural and historical environment, it does so creatively. The history of musical instruments is a history of constant invention and transformation. The flute and piano of today bear the same names as those known to J. S. Bach and Beethoven, but they do not necessarily produce the same (or even similar) sounds or play the same roles in particular sonic contexts.[1]

Spectrum photos and tone color theory now allow us to analyze the roles played by musical instruments in forming the sound shapes of a great variety of musics. We can see the spectral contribution each instrument makes to the total sound shape of any given piece; we can study the relationship of any instrument's spectral, tone color features to other structural and expressive features; we can understand the choice of a particular instrument, and of a particular instrumental sound, in any given context.

The first instrumental spectrum photo, Photo 5, shows the unique sound of the Balinese *gamelan* ensemble. It reveals how the distinctive sound of the *gamelan* originates in the spectral characteristics of its dominating instrument: the bronze-keyed, bamboo-tubed *gendèr*. Indeed, the many-layered structure of *gamelan* music and the multistrata spectrum of the *gendèr* reveal a perfect and hardly accidental fit.

The photo of the spectral formation of a late Beethoven piano sonata,

Opus 109, allows for precise analysis of the sonic differences between pianos of Beethoven's day and those of our own. Photo 6a pictures the sonata's formation as produced by a foretepiano that Beethoven himself owned. Photo 6b shows the same piece performed on a modern grand piano. Readers may be surprised by the differences revealed. With sonic analysis it is now possible for musicians to make a choice between old and new instruments based on a detailed knowledge of their sonic features and of the ways in which their sonic resources affect the expressive and structural qualities of a particular piece.

Photos 7 and 8 reveal the sonic refinement attained by two masters of early twentieth-century European music, Anton Webern and Igor Stravinsky. With these composers, each instrumental gesture and utterance reveals a distinctive spectral formation and plays a different role in the unfolding structure of the musical piece.

Photo 9, of Elliott Carter's Etude III, adds woodwind spectra to the keyboard and stringed-instrument spectra of the preceding photos. But, more important, the Etude reveals the possibility of an even more subtle level of analysis: it requires a display not only of the location of spectral elements, but also of their relative intensities—of how *much* of each spectral element is present. The presentation of instrumental spectral formations concludes with this particularly refined example.

PHOTO 5
BALINESE SHADOW-PLAY MUSIC: PEMOENGKAH (EXCERPT)
Performed by Gendèr Wayang of Kuta Village, Bali
Duration: 3 minutes 4 seconds

The sound of the Indonesian *gamelan* ensemble captivated the composers Debussy and Satie at the Paris International Exhibition of 1889. Since then it has assumed a mythical aura. *Gamelan* ensembles are now located in universities throughout the United States and Europe. Although it is impossible to hear the same performances as those heard by Debussy and Satie, we can hear recordings of those that the Canadian composer-ethnomusicologist Colin McPhee studied and transcribed in his influential writings (see Sources).

Photo 5 shows the closing part of a traditional *Pemoengkah*, recorded in 1928 in Bali. (The photo reveals some inconsistencies between the recording and McPhee's description of it.)[2] A complete *Pemoengkah*, lasting about fifteen minutes, is the prelude to a shadow play. The same piece can be played on other occasions as well. Each *Pemoengkah* consists of a number of sections; the one reproduced in Photo 5 lasts three minutes.

The unique sound of a *gamelan* ensemble grows directly out of the sound spectrum of its principal instrument, the *gendèr*. The shadow-play *gamelan*, called *gendèr wayang*, usually comprises one or more pairs of *gendèr*. A *gendèr* looks, but does not sound, like a xylophone. Each of its ten bronze keys is suspended over a tuned bamboo-tube resonator. The keys cover a

Photo 5. Balinese shadow-play music. *Pemoengkah.*

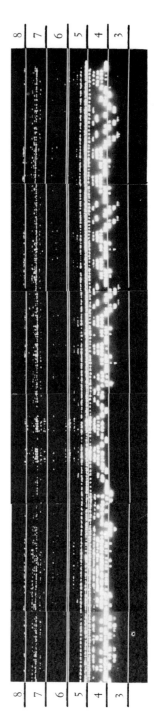

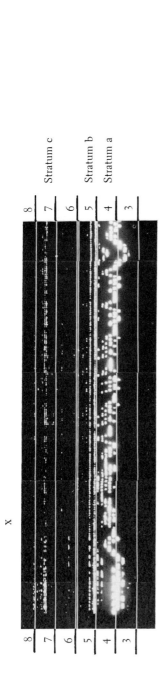

Photo 5, Details a–d.

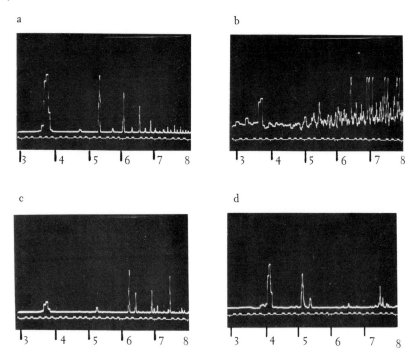

a   b

range of two octaves, five keys per octave. They are struck with a light wooden mallet that bears a round wooden disk at its tip.

Nothing could seem more simple: a metal bar struck by a wooden mallet produces a sound that is sustained by the resonance of a bamboo tube. In fact, however, the sonic linking of mallet, key, and tube produces a complex set of spectral transformations that gives rise to the multifaceted sonority of the *gendèr* and the *gamelan*. The details accompanying Photo 5 show three separate stages of transformation. Detail *a* shows the spectrum of a G$^{\sharp 3}$ key, struck by hand rather than with a wooden mallet. Activated in this way, the key produces a harmonic spectrum that strongly emphasizes the odd-numbered partials: 1, 3, 5, 7, and so on. (In electronic music this is known as a *square-wave* spectrum.) Detail *b* shows what happens when the key is struck with the *gendèr*'s wooden mallet. Throughout the range, many elements of the striking *noise* are mixed into the spectrum, most especially in registers 6, 7, and higher. Although the fundamental G$^{\sharp 3}$ is still strong, much of the remaining harmonic spectrum is swallowed up in the attack sound's noise complex.

Detail *c* is perhaps the most surprising spectrum of all. It is the sound produced by the key when it is mounted on its bamboo tube and struck by the wooden mallet; in other words, it is the actual sound of G$^{\sharp 3}$ produced by the *gendèr*. The effect of the bamboo tube is to filter out almost all of the harmonic spectrum and of the attack noise. What remains is the resonant presence of the G$^{\sharp 3}$ fundamental and a spray of spectral elements in registers

6 and 7 that derive from the attack sound. All other spectral elements of the rich sonic potential are suppressed.

Consequently, a single *gendèr* sound is always stratified into two distinct sonic regions: a resonating fundamental and a jangling "halo" far above it—the two elements separated by empty space. The exact proportions of these elements vary from note to note and from instrument to instrument, but the basic spectral configuration remains constant. It is this unusual, multiplex sound that is magnified by the presence of one or more pairs of *gendèr* to make up the unique sonority of the *gamelan* ensemble (see Photo 5).

Detail *d* allows us to examine closely the first sonority of the *Pemoeng-kah* excerpt. $C^{\#4}$ and $C^{\#5}$ are struck on the pair of *gendèr*. Far above these two fundamentals appears the spectral halo in register 7, reaching into register 8. It can be seen here, as in Detail *c* and Photo 5, that these high spectral elements are multiple: they always include several adjacent spectral elements that "rub against" each other, producing acoustic beats. This interference phenomenon is responsible for the shimmer that rings out above the *gamelan* and that produces its characteristic jangle.

Gamelan sound, then, is formed of several distinct and opposing strata. Each stratum has its own separate registral sonority. In the *Pemoengkah*, each stratum has its own speed of activity and its own distinctive sonic character.

Photo 5 shows the lowest stratum of the *Pemoengkah*, which consists of long-resonating fundamentals in registers 3 and 4. The duration of notes resonated by the bamboo tubes is always surprising.[3] A note can be sustained for more than half a minute; to shorten the notes, they must be damped by hand. This stratum shapes notes of relatively long duration, having the dull, flute-like, and [u]-like sound of fundamentals in registers 3 and 4, into a sustained "singing" melodic line (see Figure 12). In Photo 5, line 1, the many detailed undulations of this lowest stratum add up to form a single, large, curving arch of motion. It first ascends to repeated peaks in register 4 (in the middle of line 1) and then descends into register 3, before finally resettling on $C^{\#4}$ at the beginning of line 2. There is something not only flute-like but *vocal* about the way the bamboo tubes resonate these long notes into this prolonged melodic arch.

The next-higher stratum appears as the "speckled" repeating notes in register 5. These short, clanging fundamentals belong to brief, omnipresent, ostinati patterns that are divided between the right hands of the two *gendèr*. They alternate $C^{\#}$-E^5 in line 1 of Photo 5, and repeat rapid permutations of a three-note cell ($C^{\#5}$, E^5, and B^4) in line 2. This speckled stratum is higher

Fig. 12. Pemoengkah, excerpt at *x* in Photo 5, lowest stratum.

and brighter in sound and more rapid in its activity than the lowest stratum.

The highest stratum of Photo 5 is the twinkling halo of rapidly beating spectral elements in registers 7 and 8. This stratum is a constant presence, although it fluctuates in its density. It injects into the sound the fastest perceptible elements. These are acoustic beats on the order of 176 per second—which is the difference between the frequencies of $F^{\#7}$ (2,970 Hz) and G^7 (3,136 Hz). The sonority of this stratum is notable for the high, bright ring characteristic of sounds in registers 7 and 8, and by the shimmering pulsation of the pronounced rapid beats occurring between the spectral elements. Isolated from the two lower strata by a wide space, this high stratum and its tingling acoustic beats are a prominent feature of the sonic complex.

Everywhere in the *Pemoengkah* excerpt we find contrasting features superimposed on one another: the singing melody of the lowest stratum, the clanging repeated attacks of the middle stratum, and the ringing, shimmering halo of acoustic beats in the highest stratum. Rather than a succession of sonic contrasts forming an array in time, we find a simultaneity of contrasts forming a complex array in space.

As befits this particular kind of stratified structure, the evolution of the piece does not present new oppositions. Rather, it consists of moments during which one or more strata of the original sonic complex are briefly intensified or diminished. For example, line 1 intensifies the long arching melody of the lowest stratum. At x in line 1 we observe a decrease in prominence, but not the complete elimination, of the other strata. By way of contrast, the beginning of line 2 intensifies all the strata, but especially the highest stratum. Compared to line 1, register 7 is much more densely filled, and additional spectral elements reach up into register 8. As the piece unfolds, it brings various features of its constant sonic complex into sharper focus and to greater levels of intensity.

This 1928 recording, which McPhee studied, is especially interesting, for in it the sonic complex was achieved by the most limited of all Balinese instrumental ensembles: a *gamelan* of only two *gendèr*. Althouth such ensembles of two *gendèr* are not unknown, shadow-play *gendèr wayang* usually consists of four *gendèr*. *Gamelan* ensembles for other purposes can be far larger and more elaborate in their instrumental makeup. Yet all of them reproduce variations of this same unique Balinese sonic morphology—a sonic structure that reflects the distinctively stratified spectrum of its principal instument: the Balinese *gendèr*.[4]

PHOTO 6
LUDWIG VAN BEETHOVEN: PIANO SONATA IN E, OPUS 109, FIRST MOVEMENT
Performed by Jörg Demus, fortepiano (6A); Artur Schnabel, piano (6B)
Duration: 3 minutes 55 seconds (6A), 3 minutes 49 seconds (6B)

The two parts of Photo 6 allow the sonic comparison of performances on different pianos. Jörg Demus (6A) plays a *hammerflügel*, or fortepiano, made by Conrad Graf of Vienna in the year 1825. The instrument, once owned by

Photo 6, Part A. Beethoven's Piano Sonata in E, Opus 109, performed by Jörg Demus.

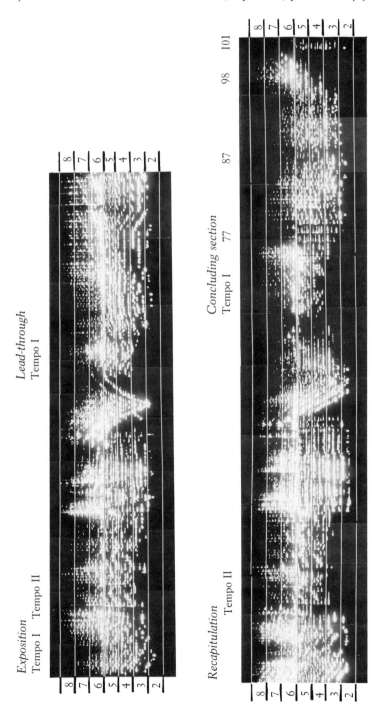

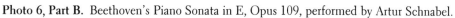

Photo 6, Part B. Beethoven's Piano Sonata in E, Opus 109, performed by Artur Schnabel.

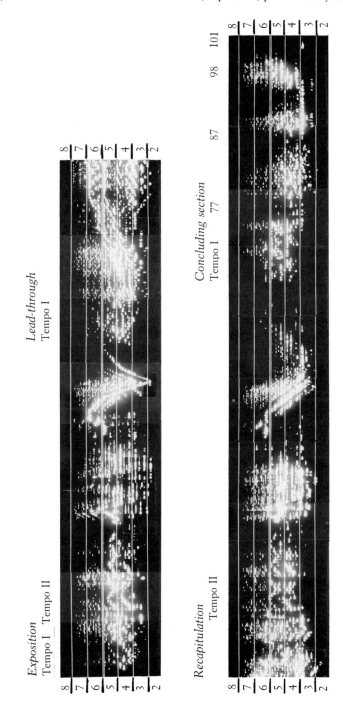

Beethoven, has been restored according to instrument-building practices of the period. Artur Schnabel's performance (6B), recorded during the 1930s, uses a modern grand piano and has, along with his other recordings of Beethoven's keyboard music, set an interpretive standard by which performances of this music can be measured.

In developing his Beethoven interpretations a half-century ago, Schnabel went to great lengths to understand Beethoven's notational specifications and to realize them in his performances. He was among the first performers to sort out the conflicting, often hidden evidence of the sketches, autograph manuscripts, and early editions. Yet there is no evidence that he searched for the instruments and instrumental sounds appropriate to Beethoven's keyboard music. Awarness of the sonic distinctiveness of historical instruments would not arrive for several decades.

Those who have heard the fortepiano of Beethoven's period deprecated as an inferior precursor of the modern grand piano may be unprepared for the sonic differences revealed by spectral analysis. Comparison of Parts A and B of Photo 6 shows that the fortepiano is consistently richer and more complex in spectrum than the modern grand piano. Other differences emerge as well. The modern piano is generally louder and its notes more efficiently damped. Compared to the sonic complexity of the fortepiano, the modern grand piano aims at the stronger projection of a simpler sonic image—a sonic simplification.

The dazzling gestures—V-shaped plunges, prolonged surges and stark oppositions—of Beethoven's registral contours appear similar in the photos. However, those of the fortepiano include, and depend upon, the presence of a high spectral register, register 8, that is considerably weaker (if not totally absent) in the corresponding sonorities of the modern grand piano. Comparison of 6A and 6B shows that in the spectral contours of the modern piano's performance, register 7 plays a role comparable to that of register 8 in the fortepiano's performance. This can be seen, for example, at the beginning of the great V-shaped plunge in line 1, and especially at the spectral crest that culminates line 1 and begins line 2 in each photo.

In addition, the fortepiano activates the lowest spectral register, register 2, to a depth and degree that is lacking in the piano. This is especially evident in the *recapitulation*, line 2, where the fortepiano dramatically opposes textures that first activate then eliminate the lowest spectral registers, 2 and 3 (measures 50–64). Both ends, the highest and the lowest, of the registral color spectrum are more fully and intensively activated by the fortepiano.

In the current debate about historical instruments, the implications of this spectral information need to be carefully considered. The implications are not entirely one-sided. Schnabel, using a modern grand piano, conveys many of the contours and oppositions of the design with exemplary clarity. On the other hand, the fortepiano of Demus (and presumably of Beethoven) manifests a degree of registral distinction, distance, and contrast that is intrinsically greater. It opposes the extended gravity of the lowest register, register 2, to the bright, sharp acuity of the highest register, 8—compared with registers 3 and 7 on the modern grand piano. In this sonata movement, by extending a similar design over approximately two additional spectral registers, the fortepiano displays a greater degree of registral tone color contrast. The spectrum photos confirm what many listeners have felt about the greater registral and timbral differentiation of the fortepiano.

And what of the movement's spectral design itself? Even at a first glance, one can easily see how it reenacts, over various spans of space and time, similar wide-sweeping gestures and motions. One might generally characterize these as wave-shaped gestures, V or inverted-V in form. In the exposition, these waves recur as a number of short successive bursts, each wave cresting higher and with increasing intensity. They culminate in the space-filling V-shaped plume in the middle of line 1. The exposition's ascending wave crests are especially noticeable in the fortepiano. They correspond to the ascending register shifts of the right hand's line as it rises through register 4 (measures 1–4), register 5 (measures 5–11), and register 6 (measures 12–14). Each wave gesture reenacts, on a scale of increasing distance and intensity, the opposition between its wave crest and trough (see Figure 13). These extraordinary registral-timbral oppositions are reflected, as well, by the exposition's opposition of extreme speeds: *vivace* and *adagio espressivo*.

In contrast to the numerous waves of the exposition, the lead-through (or development) forms a single inexorable wave that unfolds in a single tempo (see Figure 14). It surges outward from the spatial center (register 4) through the entire available space for almost thirty bars, until it reaches the spectral climax of the movement (measure 50). That climax (6A and 6B, end of line 1 and beginning of line 2) is marked by the complete and intense activation of the whole space: registers 2 through 7 (Schnabel) and registers 2 through 8 (Demus), as shown in Figure 15.

Fig. 13. Beethoven, Piano Sonata in E, first movement, Tempo II (measures 11–13).

Fig. 14. Beethoven, Piano Sonata in E, first movement, lead-through (measures 22–49).

Fig. 15. Beethoven, Piano Sonata in E, first movement, recapitulation (measures 49–53).

At this climactic apex, the pianist's hands are at the extremities of the keyboard, activating the entire spectral space of the piece. The highest and lowest spectral regions, and all the registers in between, sound simultaneously. It is there that the recapitulation and the tonal return to E major begin. We find, consequently, that Beethoven's exposition and recapitulation play dramatically opposing roles in the movement's structure. Whereas the exposition began with the piecemeal unfolding of wave gestures, the recapitulation catches the fullest and most expansive wave (that of the lead-through) at its crest. Then, until it plunges away in the middle of line 2, the recapitulation dramatically juxtaposes the very widest and narrowest spectral bands (see line 2 in 6A and 6B).

The growing drama of the exposition, lead-through and recapitulation—the growth of spectral waves to their ultimate crest, and the contrast of wave crests and wave troughs—is finally dissolved in the concluding section. The registral bands, rather than accumulating and growing, finally break up into their spectral components. Beginning with a dissolving alternation of crests and troughs (especially visible in 6B, line 2, last half), the concluding section separates into one final opposition of two disparate registral spectral bands: registers 5–8 and 2–5 (6A, measures 98–101).

Just as the exposition and recapitulation play opposing structural roles, so too do the lead-through and concluding section. The underlying symmetries of Beethoven's formal design are essential here. The exposition and recapitulation are symmetrically paired: in the former, the *vivace* and the *adagio espressivo* are both eight measures; in the latter, they are both nine measures. (Within each section the *adagio* lasts much longer than the *vivace* because of its slower tempo.) In a similar way the lead-through and concluding section are symmetrically paired: the former is thirty-three measures of *vivace*; the latter, thirty-four.

The lead-through expands and accumulates climactically, its ultimate goal being the simultaneous activation of the entire field of spectral action and colors. On the other hand, the concluding section separates its elements and dissolves post-climactically; its ultimate goal is the isolation, rather than the superposition, of the diverse colors that make up the whole. In the concluding section the wave crests are not goals, but rather are springboards back into the predominating spectral troughs—for example, the long trough at measures 77–87 in 6A and 6B. The shape of Beethoven's gestures—indeed, the intense structural drama of this movement—depends upon such oppositions of spectrum and register, just as it does upon those of contrasting tempi and tonalities.

The extensions of the piano's range during Beethoven's lifetime offered the composer an increasing space for motion and for sonic exploration. (Or was it sonic explorations of composers like Beethoven which compelled instrument makers to enlarge the range of their instruments?) This sonata movement requires an additional half-register upward (in register 6) and one additional step downward (in register 1), compared to the pianos and piano compositions of Beethoven's early career. In this movement, the expanded pianistic space frames the entire structure. It is toward the newly available notes, E^1 at the bottom and B^6 at the top, and toward their extreme spectral partials, that the structure is propelled as it forms the dramatic oppositions of registral color lying at its expressive and sonic core.

Nowhere else in his music did Beethoven shape powerful expressive and sonic oppositions so concisely. The oppositions determine the placement of every sonic detail and are reflected, as we have seen, in the play of tempi and in the play of registral colors. The formal traditions of the sonata have been reconceived so that formerly parallel entities, such as exposition and recapitulation, are transformed into directly opposing entities. Indeed, the most obvious traditional parallelism of all, the literal repetition of the exposition, is entirely eliminated. The lead-through and concluding section emerge, too, as opposing entities. No place remains in the structure for holding back the on-going processes of transformation and opposition. The changing wave gestures follow one another ceaselessly, forming the larger stages of growth, accumulation, climax, and dissolution that constitute a single overriding wave—which is, finally, the structure of the entire movement.[5]

PHOTO 7
IGOR STRAVINSKY: THREE PIECES FOR STRING QUARTET, PIECE II
Performed by the Parrenin String Quartet
Duration: 2 minutes 28 seconds

No composer possesses a more distinctive sonic fingerprint than Igor Stravinsky.[6] Certain textures have become instantly recognizable as Stravinskian: a bright, clear, high sonority, often sustained; an array of sharp pulsations, often (but not always) dense and dark-hued; the built-up attack of a single sound, whose continuation then hangs "disembodied" after the pronounced attack.

Photo 7 substantiates these sonic impressions. The spectral range activated in the photo immediately reveals the physical source of the bright, clear sonority. Again and again Stravinsky's sounds generate substantial spectral content up through register 9 (see e^1, f, g, i, and k in the photo). Since the next octave higher, register 10 (16,000–32,000 Hz), exceeds the normal range of human hearing, Stravinsky's sounds are intensely active to the highest limits of audibility. By comparison, many of the preceding photos reveal little activation of these high spectral regions.

Stravinsky makes use of the lowest registers, too. The spectral range is active down through register 2, the cello's lowest register and, consequently, the lowest register normally available to the string quartet (see Photo 7, a, d, f, and i).

Especially important for Stravinskian sonority are the relationships between the lowest and highest spectral registers. Only rarely does the lowest register sustain; especially, it does not sustain and mix with the highest registers except under special conditions; rather, touches of the lowest registers precede moments in the highest spectral registers, or vice versa. Again and again, registral extremes are alternated—the grave directly opposed to the acute, as in Photo 7, a/b (see Figure 16 and Details a and b). Similar directly contrasting juxtapositions can be seen at dd^1/ee^1 (measures 15–17), and around f (measures 20–23). In each instance, a grave spectral region stretching down into register 2 is juxtaposed with an acute spectral region reaching up into register 9.

Given the continuing opposition of spectral extremes, it is fitting that the two climactic gestures of the piece (Photo 7, i and i^1) both consist of the immediate juxtaposition of the lowest and highest registers in a single motion that rips upward through the entire spectral range, registers 2–9 (see Figure 17).

Photo 7. Stravinsky, *Three Pieces for String Quartet*, Piece II.

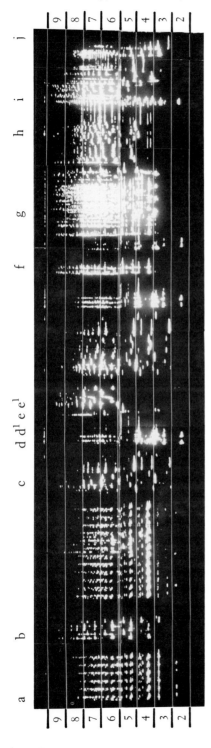

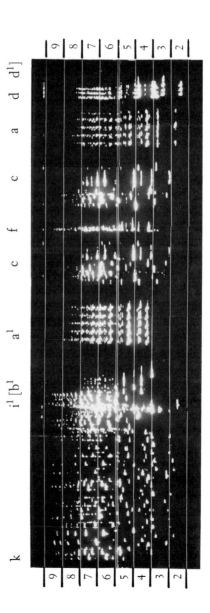

Fig. 16. Stravinsky, *Three Pieces for String Quartet*, Piece II, opposing spectral areas *a* (measures 1–3) and *b* (measures 4–5).

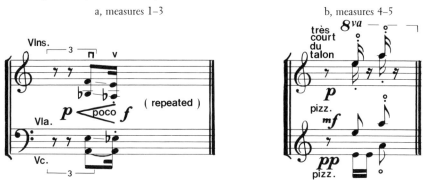

Fig. 17. Stravinsky, *Three Pieces for String Quartet*, Piece II, climactic gesture *i* (measure 33).

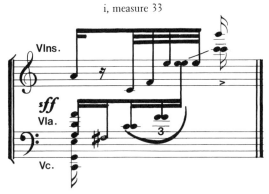

It was Edward Cone who first suggested *stratification* as the characteristic organizing principle of Stravinsky's musical thought.[7] Pozzi Escot and I have shown that the rhythmic activity of this quartet piece is organized in distinct *pulsation strata.*[8] Now it appears that stratification, too, describes the piece's design of spectral, registral colors. The spectral registral method is similar to that used by such a Neo-Impressionist painter as Seurat in creating intense hue sensations: side-by-side juxtaposition of complementary contrasts, rather than simultaneous mixing of colors.[9] Over and over, spectra are focused in brief, dot-like moments of opposing grave and acute strata. The isolation and juxtaposition of opposing color strata play a primary role in Stravinsky's color design.

Stravinsky's spectral formations are distinctive, as well, in the ways in which they distribute spectral density, both in time and in space. This gives rise to a new pair of oppositions: that of sound and silence, and that of high-density and low-density spectral formations.

In the music of Webern, Stravinsky's contemporary, silence is a recog-

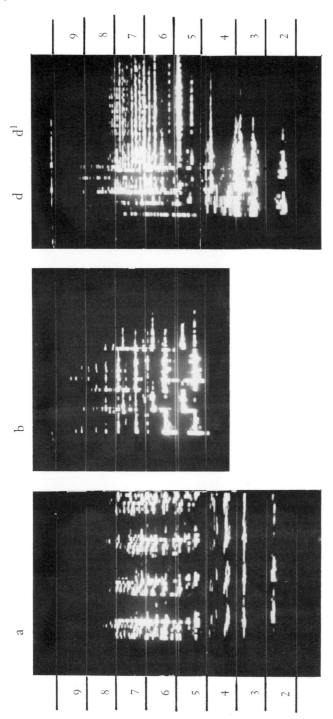

nized formative musical element; Photo 7 reveals that it plays a crucial role in the Stravinskian texture as well. Whereas Webern's is large-scale silence, Stravinsky's is small-scale—the constant accumulation of small bits of silence that envelop almost every sonic moment (compare Photos 7 and 8). In its totality, however, the silence is as great and vital in Stravinsky as in Webern. It is the necessary precondition for Stravinskian sound and leads to a vivid characteristic of Stravinsky's sonic fingerprint: the distinctive formation of the moment of sonic *onset*, or *attack*—that instant, often explosive, when a silence and its succeeding sound meet. Stravinsky repeatedly dramatizes that juncture by composing a massive spectral attack that intrudes into the silence, and almost as instantaneously subsides into near-silence—with only one or a few spectral strands left dangling from the dense attack (see d/d^1 in Photo 7 and the corresponding detail).

At each of these junctures there is, first, the density opposition of silence and sound. The attack moment adds a host of additional spectral oppositions: rich/sparse, wide/narrow, loud/soft, and clipped/sustained. Following the onset and release, the texture often reverts to silence and the sonic cycle immediately begins anew.

The musical score testifies to Stravinsky's inventiveness in precisely shaping the onset moment of the sonic envelope. Every onset is specifically conceived and notated, whether it is bowed (*arco*) or plucked (*pizzicato*); both bowed *and* plucked; upbow or downbow; at the bow's tip or at its heel; with slides (*glissando*) into or out of an attack, or level; sustained or immediately clipped off.

In the photo and details, we can observe the interplay of spectral densities. In Details *a* and *b*, drawn from the first and second phrases of the piece, we see that those phrases form two opposing sonority areas, each of which is characterized by three different kinds of spectral opposition that reinforce one another: registral, density, and onset opposition.

The dense, grave sonorities of area *a* activate as many as twenty simultaneous partials covering six different registers, registers 2–7. By contrast, the sparse, acute sonorities of area *b* (two whole octaves higher, registers 4–9) hardly activate more than ten simultaneous partials over a comparable six-register space, and that number only at the instant of attack. As the second texture shifts the focus upward, it reduces the spectral density by more than half. Area *a*, grave and rich, is doubly opposed to area *b*, which is acute and sparse. The registral contrast is paralleled and magnified by the density contrast.

A closer look at the details reveals the specific onset opposition that further characterizes *a* and *b*. In area *a*, each repeated gesture shows spectral growth from onset to release. Each sonority in area *b*, with its onset reinforced by pizzicato attack, reverses this spectral design: each reveals spectral decay from onset to release. Thus, each sonority is a highly shaped sonic event set off by surrounding silence. Each area of sonorities achieves strong sonic character through the combination of several spectral sonic features:

area *a* is grave and rich, with a swelling onset; area *b* is acute and sparse, with a decaying onset.

We find here, as elsewhere, that the beginning sonic features of a piece—whether of register, density, or onset—act as sonic gestures or themes. Each has important consequences in the ensuing structure of the piece. As the musical work unfolds and its textures evolve (often toward greater complexity), the original, essential sonic characteristics remain clearly discernible.

In Photo 7 we can observe how the passage *de* condenses and combines in a new form sonic features already presented in *ab*:

	e—acute, rich /e^1—acute, sparse
d—grave, rich/d^1—grave, sparse	

Between *d* and *e* the opposition of spectral registers, grave/acute, is intensified (for example, d^1 falls in registers 3–6, e^1 in registers 6–9). At the same time, between *d* and d^1 and again between *e* and e^1 the opposition rich/sparse is recreated. Compared to *a* and *b*, we find here a briefer and more complex combinatorial opposition of the sonic features.

The piece's textures attain their most extended sonic complexity in its two opposing climactic central panels, *g* and *k* in Photo 7. Both panels cover wide spectral ranges and include a great variety of spectral colors. Indeed, *k* activates registers 2–9, all eight of the spectral registers that are heard in the piece, and is the only extended span that does so. Nonetheless, *g* and *k* stand in vivid opposition to each other. Whereas *g* is spectrally as dense and active as possible, *k* is much sparser in spectral distribution across its very wide range. Consequently, *g* and *k* recreate on the largest scale the initial density opposition rich/sparse.

Panel *k* is a marvelous example of the way in which bits of sound and silence, when combined, air out a complicated texture. In this texture Stravinsky uncharacteristically superimposes in a single mosaic the highest and lowest spectral registers and all those in between. He also combines within it many different kinds of plucked and bowed onsets. Because the texture is so thoroughly aired by silences, the entire play of diverse sonorities sounds with utter transparency. Every register from 2 to 9, and every onset from plucked to bowed, plays directly off of every other one, and each resounds against the silences that envelop and articulate them all. The result is a novel conception of musical climax, at once playful and sonically diverse.

Having combined within these two climactic passages the full range of registers, densities, and attacks, Stravinsky closes the piece by recalling its original sonically opposing gestures. He does this, too, in an inventive way (see Photo 7, line 2, last half). The original textures are reordered: below the characteristic Stravinskian spectral presence in the highest registers (5 and above) the lower regions (registers 4, 3, and 2, at a^1, *c*, *a*, and *d*) are successively mixed in. We are given one last reminder of the piece's generating sonic contrasts, and one last imprint of Stravinsky's oppositional sonic strata.[10]

PHOTO 8

ANTON WEBERN: FOUR PIECES FOR VIOLIN AND PIANO, OPUS 7, PIECES III AND IV
Performed by Isaac Stern, violin, and Charles Rosen, piano
Duration: 1 minute 18 seconds (Piece III), 1 minute (Piece IV)

In a well-known accolade, Stravinsky likened Webern to a diamond cutter—"cutting out his diamonds, his dazzling diamonds, the mines of which he had such a perfect knowledge."[11] Photo 8 reveals that those mines extend to the depths of musical sound. The photo reveals two facets of Webern's precise sonic distinction. First, each sound (or sonic phrase) appears to be a specific and unique creation, with its own spectrum and registral placement and its own individual hue and value, unlike those of any other sound or sonic moment of the musical work. At the same time, the sonic aggregate formed by each piece—each complete context of sounds—is also a specific and unique creation.

Everywhere in this book we observe sonic exactitude in music, to a degree that was previously unexpected. This is true with respect both to individual sonic moments and to the larger sonic formations that are the products of those moments. What appears different in Webern is the rigor of transformation: every new moment represents, for him, a *new* facet of the sonic essence. The large sonic formation must be conceived so that it contains and generates only *changing* facets of that sonic essence. Webern expanded on the theory of perpetual variation developed by his mentor, Schoenberg, and transposed it to the sonic realm. When we compare Webern with Stravinsky in this respect, we find that Stravinsky, too, was a creator of extraordinary sonic moments. However, in his larger sonic formations he was not averse to repetition. Indeed, he depended upon it as a way of creating new sonic oppositions.

Pieces III and IV of Webern's Opus 7 illustrate his personal method. Photo 8 reveals that these two pieces are diametrically opposed sonic structures. The third piece—sparse, registrally limited, low-lying, gradually accumulating density—is opposed in each of these respects to the fourth piece—which is massive, registrally extended, high-soaring, and gradually dissolving in density. With this wide gamut of oppositions so rigorously pursued, Webern evokes a great range of sonic space and colors, and does so with his usual radical economy of strokes. Each piece unfolds its sonic essence and its entire world of sonic transformations in hardly more than a minute.

The beginning of each piece announces the intense contrasting drama of these few sounds (see Figure 18). The muted, scarcely audible, unchanging single note of the low violin in Piece III is starkly opposed to the unmuted, violently accented barrage of loud, widely scattered violin notes in IV. The scarcely perceptible, limited spectrum of the one opposes the wide, complex, intense spectrum of the other. The spectral contrast of the violin is reinforced by a parallel contrast in the piano. The barely audible, single-note attacks of the piano in III and the dense sonic mass of IV oppose each other in the same way.

Photo 8. Anton Webern, Four Pieces for Violin and Piano, Pieces III and IV.

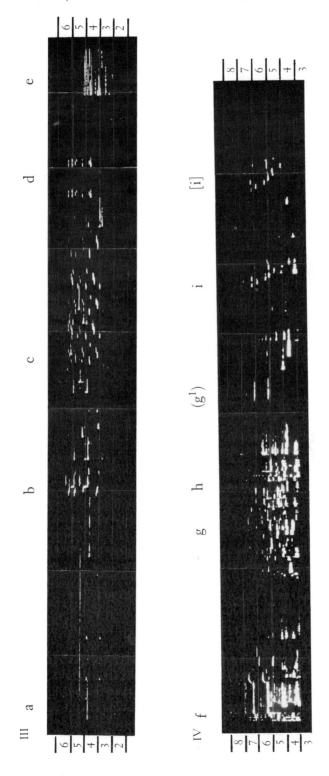

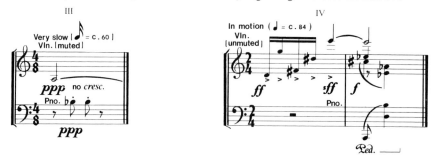

Fig. 18. Webern, *Four Pieces for Violin and Piano,* beginning of Pieces III and IV.

To achieve his sonic transformations within and between pieces, Webern requires from the violinist a different instrumental performance technique at every moment. The violin is not conceived as a single constant tone color, but rather as the source of a variety of contrasting spectral qualities:

Piece III

a. Muted, sustained single note, *ppp*—the sparsest violin spectrum in the piece (*a* in Photo 8).
b. Muted, on the bridge (*sul ponticello*)—a "glassy" sonority produced by bowing close to the bridge while muted, a technique that enriches a limited range of upper partials (especially partials 2, 3, and 4; see *b* in Photo 8).
c. Muted, bowing with the wood of the bow (*col legno*)—using the wood rather than the hairs of the bow, muted, complicates the harmonic spectrum with inharmonic, or noise, elements (*c* in photo 8).
d. Muted undulation, on the bridge—the most complex spectrum, the result of an overlapping undulation of two glassy spectra (*d* in Photo 8).

The thirty-three muted notes of the violin in this third piece represent a sonic *tour de force.* The notated pitches ($G^{\#3}$–B^4) hardly exceed a single octave in the violin's lowest register, and never exceed the dynamic of *ppp*. Still, each sound is spectrally different, and each plays a specific role in a cumulative progression toward ever more rich, complex violin spectral formations. Even muted, in a single register, and at a single *ppp* dynamic, the violin is not a single tone color. Rather, it is the source of an orderly progression of diverse hues and values, depending upon specific performance techniques brought into play by the composer and performer.

Although it might seem that the piano is sonically less malleable, it undergoes a parallel sonic transformation from ultra-sparse to rich. Beginning with the very short, quasi-plucked single notes *ppp*, it progresses to sustained sonorities of one, two, three, and finally six notes. The last and densest sonority of the movement (Photo 8e) is formed of six simultaneous notes, two of which quickly undulate in tremolo. Photo 8 shows the complexity of this culminating spectrum. The increasing density of the notated piano textures, their registral placement, and the tremolo (which continually reactivates the partials) all contribute to the piano's progression from spectral simplicity to complexity.

Consequently, the violin and piano spectra undergo parallel transformations. As the piece unfolds, each becomes spectrally richer and more complex. Together, they create the ongoing spectral accumulation displayed in Photo 8, line 1. Without spectrum analysis it would be difficult to discern the similarity of the sonic transformations of the violin and piano, which are arrived at by entirely different means on the two instruments.

Still, all of its internal transformation, growth, and accumulation notwithstanding, Piece III unfolds within a sparse, limited, low-lying spectral framework. The muted violin does not leave its lowest regions, in space or dynamics. Partials hardly extend above the lower half of register 6, and are largely limited to registers 2–5. The constant, systematic spectral transformation is accomplished with gradations that are extremely subtle and fine.

We have already seen that with its very first sounds, Piece IV contrasts dramatically with Piece III. The violin's initial gesture, bursting upward, unmuted, frees all of its previously repressed spectral brilliance. It drives up from register 4 to its new locus in register 6, with intense spectral activity reaching up through register 8, and higher. (Notice that while the photo of Piece III covers registers 2–6, that of Piece IV is shifted upward to reveal the newly activated spectral regions in registers 7 and 8.) The spectra, intensified by the new ff dynamic, shatter the previous registral limits. The fundamentals and spectra of the violin and piano together momentarily activate an enormous range stretching from register 1 to register 8, a span covering eight of the ten humanly audible registers. The opposition to Piece III could hardly be more vivid.

Yet, as in Piece III, the violin in Piece IV progresses through a set of changing performance techniques and spectral transformations. In contrast to Piece III, Piece IV progresses from high to low spectral density:

Piece IV

f. Unmuted sustained notes—first strongly attacked ff, with a rich, brilliant spectrum; then less strongly attacked and increasingly quiet (f in Photo 8).

g. Unmuted harmonics—the harmonics bring a radical reduction in spectral richness; they, too, generally progress from strongly attacked to sustained and quiet (compare Photo 8, g and g^1).

h. Unmuted pizzicato—plucked violin sounds eliminate virtually all sustained spectral complexity (h in Photo 8).

i. Unmuted, on the bridge (*sul ponticello*)—so high and soft ("like a whisper" is the composer's command) that only a hint of previous spectral complexity is evoked (i in Photo 8).

Here, too, as in Piece III, the violin's sonic transformations are paired with changing piano densities and dynamics. The loud seven-note simultaneities with which the piano begins the piece are reduced to sustained single notes, *ppp*, by the piece's end. As in Piece III, the combination of the two instruments creates a large-scale spectral transformation: in this case, the unmistakable spectral dissolution shown in Photo 8, line 2.

We now realize that each moment in the two pieces—indeed, each violin performance technique and piano density—is sonically distinct and unique. However, taken together, the sounds of the two instruments, and their spectral formations, reflect one another. Both instruments contribute, in tandem, to the contrasting structural processes of the pieces. Like sonic mirrors or many-faceted diamonds, the two instruments and two pieces form flashing reflections of each other.[12]

PHOTO 9
ELLIOTT CARTER: EIGHT ETUDES AND A FANTASY, ETUDE III
Performed by the New England Conservatory Scholarship Woodwind Quartet
Duration: 1 minute

Two of Elliott Carter's eight etudes pose a challenge to prevailing assumptions about the nature of musical analysis and understanding: "With the composition of [Etude VII] in 1950, one could say that music no longer consists merely of *motion*, or *change*, of fundamental pitches. The piece defies analysis where analysis is dependent (as it almost always has been) upon such motion."[13] This comment applies equally to Etude III. Regarded from the standpoint of earlier music, the two etudes appear to be utterly static and unchanging. Etude VII seems to consist of only a single note, G^4; Etude III seems to consist of only a single fixed major triad—D, $F^\#$, A in register 4. The only apparent activity within Etude III is the rhythmic rotation of the triadic notes among the instruments of a woodwind quartet. As with Etude VII, in order to understand the shaping of Etude III we must probe below a surface formed of unchanging notated pitches.

Indeed, Etude III requires especially subtle probing. In modeling its sonic transformations, we must carry our analysis beyond the spectrum photos. In such photos Etude III reveals hardly more than a single continuous spectrum, made up of unchanging (or little changing) partials of the three generating fundamentals. It is only when we observe the changing relative *quantities*, or intensities, of the constant partials that the etude's patterns of transformation appear. Such an analysis is provided by the details in three parts of Photo 9. From the spectral sampling of eighteen chosen moments, an unsuspected structure of sonic relationships emerges.

The structure of the entire etude is foreshadowed in the first phrase (Details *a–h* in Part A). In Figure 19 we can see how the first phrase passes the triadic notes among the four woodwinds—at first slowly (half notes), then more rapidly (quarter notes, in the box), and finally again at the original pace. Just as there emerges a transformation of the rhythmic pace of instrumental change, so too there emerges a spectral transformation as the phrase unfolds. The initial spectrum (Detail *a*) concentrates its elements in the lowest spectral registers of the etude, registers 4 and 5. Only two partials of significance

Photo 9. Elliott Carter, Etude III. Part A, Details *a–h.*

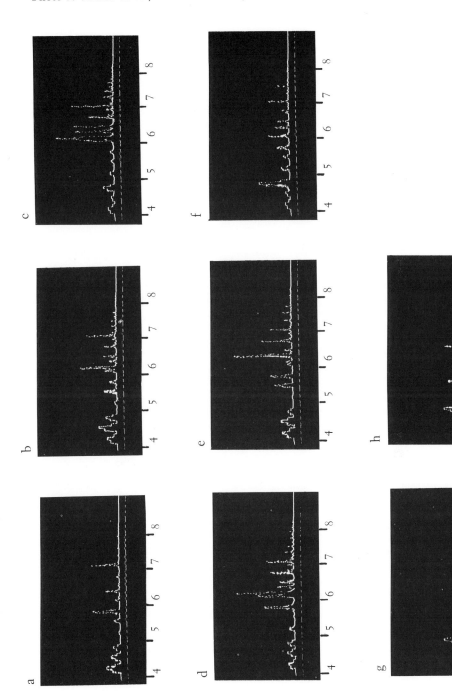

Photo 9, Part B, Details a–e.

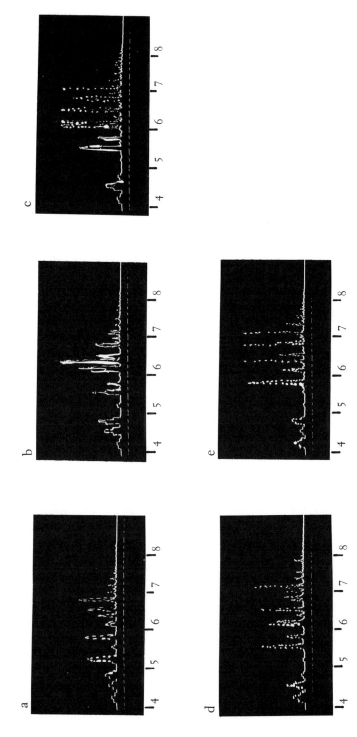

Photo 9, Part C, Details a–e.

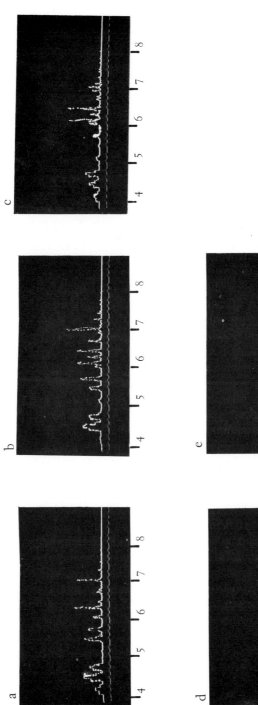

Fig. 19. Carter, Etude III, instrumental fluctuations at the beginning. The letters *a–h* correspond to Details *a–h* in Photo 9, Part A.

	a	b	c	d	e	f	g	h
A^4:	⌈Fl⌋	− Fl −	− Fl	Bn	Ob	Cl	− −Cl− −	⌈Cl⌉
$F^{\#4}$:	|Bn⌋	− Bn	Cl− −	Cl	Bn	Ob	− −Ob	|Fl|
D^4:	⌊Cl|	Ob − − Ob− −		Ob	Cl	Bn	Fl	⌊Bn⌋

♩ ♩ ♩ ♩ ♩ ♩ ♩ ♩

Fl = Flute   Ob = Oboe

Cl = Clarinet   Bn = Bassoon

appear in the higher registers, 6 and 7. However, as the phrase continues, the spectral energy shifts markedly upward to registers 6 and 7 (Details *b–e*). Each of the sonorities in *b–e* reveals at least four partials of significance in registers 6 and 7. Indeed, it is in those registers that the bulk of spectral energy is concentrated, while the spectral intensities in registers 4 and 5 are relatively diminished.

Consequently, embedded in the first phrase is a fleeting, subtle suggestion of a spectral shift from the more grave to the more acute registers, and from a narrower, sparser spectral concentration to a wider, richer spectral spread. This hint of sonic transformation is borne by spectra and rhythms working together. As the spectra ascend and widen, the durations diminish from half notes to quarter notes. At the phrase's end, with the return of half-note durations, the spectra recede again to the original concentrations in registers 4 and 5 (Details *f–h*). In these last details there is a marked reduction in both the number and intensity of spectral elements in registers 6 and 7 compared to the preceding sonorities, *b–e*. In this phrase, then, the spectral and rhythmic transformations move in tandem, if not in absolute synchrony. Neither change of pitches (which are always D-F$^{\#}$-A in register 4) nor change of dynamic (which is always *p*) plays a part.

There are two specific instrumental agents of the spectral transformation that occurs in this initial phrase: the flute and the oboe. In their spectra we find crystallized the spectral opposition of the entire phrase. The flute (on the triadic notes, *p*) activates partials in registers 4 and 5, without any intense higher partials. On the other hand, the oboe, and only the oboe among these instruments, activates significant spectral elements and energy in registers 6 and 7 on the triadic notes, *p*. Consequently, it is the withdrawal of the flute, which is entirely missing from the boxed-in central quarter notes of the phrase (Figure 19), and the appearance of the oboe, which is missing from the framing outer sonorities (broken boxes), that combine to effect the sonic transformation revealed in the spectral details.

Elliott Carter may have been thinking of such a phrase when he wrote: "The entrance, register, sound of an oboe must be a matter of formal and expressive signification for the whole piece. The combination of instruments is as much a compositional consideration as the material they play, and all must reflect the overall intention."[14] When we observe this initial pattern of spectral transformation, we can understand why the disappearance of the flute and the appearance of the oboe are of such importance in the context of this phrase.

Still, we do not yet understand the full significance of the first phrase: that is revealed only with the complete unfolding of the etude. Indeed the principal formal and sonic event of the etude is yet to come. That event, the crescendo of all four woodwind instruments in measures 9–11, gradually raises the notated dynamic level from *p* to *mf*.

The spectral transformation produced by this prolonged crescendo is shown in Details *a–e* of Part B. Astonishingly, it appears as a still more intense variation of the spectral levitation produced by the flute disappearance and oboe appearance in the first phrase. The precise foreshadowing role of the first phrase now becomes clear. As in the center of that phrase, throughout the crescendo numerous partials in registers 6 and 7 become steadily stronger. At the same time, the fundamentals in register 4 become progressively weaker (*a–e*). Because of this spectral growth upward, the sound of the woodwind quartet at its climax (as in a truly spectral illusion) seems to rise on its own power into a higher octave. It is a magical moment.

At this spectral climax, too, rhythmic durations and spectral elements, as well as the dynamic changes, collaborate to produce the total effect of the moment. The extended rhythmic durations (half notes to whole notes) and the general crescendo both serve to reinforce in a climactic way this spectral transsubstantiation. The fleeting foreshadowing of sonic transformation in the first phrase here receives its full realization.

Spectrum analysis provides a tool whereby the important similarity of these passages—the initial one characterized by instrumental change and rhythmic diminution, the climactic one by dynamic change and rhythmic augmentation—can be discovered and shown. Remove the spectral features and the most critical formal links of the entire etude (the first phrase's internal spectral opposition that prefigures the ultimate opposition between the etude's beginning, climax, and ending) disappear. Without spectral understanding, the link between the successive transformations—instrumental, rhythmic, and dynamic—would evaporate: it is the spectral transformations that the instrumental and dynamic changes, together, serve to create.

After the dynamic spectral climax (Part B, *c–e*, measures 11–12), a rapid transitional diminuendo brings all of the variable parameters back to their original states. In almost every respect (dynamic, rhythmic, instrumental) the beginning is exactly restated in measures 12 (last half) and 13. Details *a–c* in Part C show, therefore, a necessary spectral resemblance to the original formations of Details *a–c* in Part A. (In the performance analyzed, this resemblance holds for Details *a* and *b*. The third sonority, *c*, is not played consistently in the two passages. Spectrum analysis is a pitiless observer of performance.)

Although this final phrase of Etude III begins identically to the first phrase, it ends differently. The crucial feature of the ending is not spectral growth and ascent; rather, it is spectral reduction and descent (Details *d* and *e* in part C). The closing phrase diminishes from *p* to *più p* (yet softer). This dynamic transformation concentrates the closing spectral elements in register 4. It wipes out virtually all of the higher spectral regions summoned up in the prior transformations and in the original sonorities. Consequently, this concluding phrase is a mirror image, a spectral inversion, of the prior transformations. In the repeated alternations of the closing sonorities (*d* and *e*) the interplay between acute and grave transformations is highlighted, as the oboe first joins and then withdraws from the closing, fading sound.

We noted at the beginning of this commentary that, in the light of earlier analytic methods, this etude could emerge only as incomprehensible, static, or both. It now, however, reveals itelf to be a set of succinct, precise spectral formations whose roles and relationships, whether of identity or opposition, are clear at every instant.

Most clearly revealed is the subtlety of Etude III's sonic transformations. In order to manifest themselves, they require the most precise performance, measurement, and perception; and, of course, prior to these steps they required equally precise and imaginative composition. Evident in the etude are the impressive speed and concision with which Carter develops his structure. The whole set of sonic identities and transformations requires exactly one minute to unfold. This speed and concision draw attention to an intrinsic characteristic of sound spectra, and of music whose structural source is in spectral formations. It is true that all spectra require some time for sounding and hearing. However, they are, especially by comparison with such musical features as melodic lines and tonal progressions, fleeting phenomena. They allow, as in Carter's etude or in the examples by Stravinsky and Webern, for the creation of rich and subtle sonic forms which at the same time display an exemplary concentration. A minute is time enough to reveal a whole spectral world.[15]

3.
Large Mixed Ensembles

BY COMBINING THE tone colors and spectral resources of many different instruments, or of human voices and instruments, the musical imagination has
been able to achieve some of its most varied expressive and structural designs.
In Photos 10–14 we see, in works ranging from Mozart's Requiem
K. 626 to Edgard Varèse's *Hyperprism*, some examples of the dazzling diversity of sound shapes and tone color formations that composers and performers have created.

The "Confutatis" of Mozart's Requiem and a long excerpt from the
"Tibi omnes angeli" of Berlioz's Te Deum are depicted in Photos 10 and 11.
Here voices and instruments combine to create a pair of striking sound
shapes. Mozart's is operatic in its sudden opposition of sonic characteristics,
resembling conflicting characters in a drama. Berlioz, on the other hand, folds
his spectral oppositions into a gradually evolving sonic textural progression of
great scope and power.

Photos 12 and 13 are purely orchestral. Photo 12 is of "Nuages"
("Clouds"), one of Debussy's Nocturnes for orchestra. Photo 13 is of the
climactic moment in Alban Berg's opera *Wozzeck*. In many ways, the sound
shapes of these examples mirror the shapes of the Mozart and Berlioz pieces.
Like Mozart, Berg is vivid in his dramatic, theatrical opposition of sonic characteristics. Debussy, like Berlioz, weaves his many spectral transformations
into a gradually evolving sonic tapestry of great subtlety.

The spectrum photos reveal not only underlying similarities, but also the
unique shape of each piece. The Mozart and Berg structures both resemble
and oppose each other. The Berg accumulates tension and spectral, sonic
complexity. In Mozart the same properties suddenly, or gradually, dissipate
and expire. Similarly, the Berlioz reveals an evolving progressive accumulation of spectral density and complexity. The Debussy, on the other hand, reveals the progressive dissolution of these same sonic qualities. Each different
design achieves its ultimate shape and expressive force by integrating the varied spectral, sonic qualities of a large ensemble of participants. Diverse voices
and instruments, language features and musical features—all join together to
produce the resulting sonic structures.

The ensemble of Varèse's *Hyperprism* includes nine brass and woodwind instruments, as well as a large and diverse battery of percussion instru-

ments. The nature of percussion sound and its contribution to music's structural and sonic shapes has been one of the least studied and least understood elements of musical analysis. This is especially odd in view of the fact that, next to the human voice, percussion instruments are the most widely used in the world. Photo 14 enables us to understand the percussion sounds of *Hyperprism*. We can analyze their specific relationships to its wind instrument sounds, and the many contributions both make to the structural design of the whole. We can now directly see the formations of those *sound masses* of which Varèse was such a visionary explorer.

PHOTO 10
Wolfgang Amadeus Mozart: Requiem K. 626, "Confutatis"

Performed by the chorus and orchestra of the Gulbenkian Foundation of Lisbon; Michael Corboz, Conductor

Duration: 2 minutes 55 seconds

Confutatis maledictis,	When the damned are confronted,
flammis acribus addictis,	sentenced to searing flames,
voca me cum benedictis.	call me with the blessed.
Oro supplex et acclinis,	I plead, supplicant and bent,
cor contritum quasi cinis,	heart crushed like ashes—
gere curam mei finis!	watch over my end!

These six lines of the Requiem Mass for the dead—with their opposing visions of the damned and the blessed, the dead and the living—encapsulate the intrinsic drama of the sacred ritual. Mozart, the quintessential dramatic composer, makes the textual oppositions the basis of the entire musical, sonic structure. For example, the initial two lines, which speak of "the damned," are presented solely by *low*-register performing forces: men's tenor and bass choral voices, the cellos and basses of the *basso continuo,* and (in Süssmayr's probably spurious orchestral completion)[1] trombones with bassoons. The following line of "the blessed" is, in contrast, presented solely by *high*-register performing forces: women's (or boy's) choral voices and violins alone, without other supporting elements. Photo 10 shows, in line 1, the resulting blatant spectral textural contrasts, twice presented by the opposing forces, their words and music.

Photo 10 reveals, too, that the oppositions of Mozart's sonic structure are not quite as simple as the schematic layout of the scoring—damned/blessed equaling low/high—might suggest. While the notated fundamentals of the first phrase, "the damned . . . sentenced to searing flames," appear only in the lower registers (registers 1–4), the total texture activates additional partials which flare up throughout registers 5, 6, and 7 (Photo 10, line 1, first quarter). Not just the lowest registers, but rather the entire audible range up to register 8 is packed with spectral intensity. The high spectral elements are especially presented and reinforced by the high formant of the many acute [i] vowels sung by the men. Repeatedly, [i], whose register 7 resonance is the highest of any Latin vowel, resounds in the text. Its seven recur-

Photo 10. Mozart, Requiem K. 626, "Confutatis."

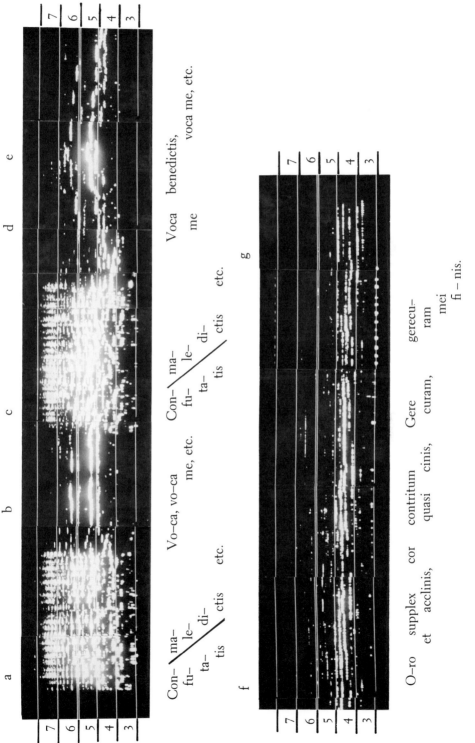

rences in the phrase's sixteen syllables greatly outnumber the appearance of any other vowel: "Confutat*is* maled*i*ct*is* / flamm*is* ac*ri*bus add*i*ct*is*." Furthermore, Mozart repeats the words dominated by this vowel, while the seldom-repeated word ("confutatis") is saturated with low vowel formants: [o], [u], and [a].

While their fundamentals are located in the lower registers, all of the sounds of the first phrase—men's voices repeating the vowel [i], and low-register strings playing *f*—are rich in high spectral elements. These spectral elements repeatedly rise up (an imaginative observer might say "like flames") through the entire spectral space of Photo 10.

We have already observed that the spectral contrast in the first and second phrases of Photo 10 is unmistakable. To the wide-flaring, dense, rich, repeatedly attacked spectra of the first phrase (the "damned"), the second phrase (the "blessed") opposes the sparse, widely spaced, sustained spectra shown in the photo. As they draw inward from registers 1–7, the spectra of the second phrase thin out radically. The women's (or boys'), voices softly reiterate the words "voca me" ("call me"), withdrawing the acute [i] of the first phrase. So, too, the instrumentation withdraws the highest and lowest spectral elements. The spatially extreme elements and the intense, feverish activity of the first phrase's spectral formation have entirely disappeared. It is by this radical spectral and sonic *purification* of many features, rather than merely the spectral contrast grave/acute, that the textual opposition "damned/blessed" is actually presented musically.

Despite their variation of other musical details, the third and fourth phrases recreate the same textual and sonic oppositions as the first and second. In the fourth phrase, in a particularly striking variant, the single word "benedictis" ("blessed") is spectrally enriched for a brief moment at the linear and spectral peak. This can be seen in line 1 of Photo 10 and in Figure 20. There, with the women singing in subdued voices (*sotto voce*), we find another instance of acute [i]'s, which, together with acute [ε]'s (both drawn from the word "bened*i*ct*is*"), activate *high* spectral regions. With the immediate return of the high voices to the repeated phrase "voca me," these momentary bright spectral lights are once again extinguished.

Since the dramatic contrasts of the first half of the "Confutatis" have been so clearly spelled out in the spectral view, we can now ask what role the last half of the movement, the prayer "I plead, supplicant and bent," plays in the unfolding structural and expressive design.

The long chromatic descending sequences of the upper voice of the second half (Photo 10, line 2) surely rank among Mozart's most unusual and moving melodic-harmonic constructions (see Figure 21). No less striking is the line's absolutely organic derivation from the third and fourth phrases of line 1. The way it chromatically fills in the space from A to E and the many details of its contour are prefigured by the cadential bass-line descent of phrase 3 (see Figure 22). Furthermore, its long descending line formed of falling suspensions tied over bar-lines derives directly from the "benedictis" peak of phrase 4, as does the specific rhythm of its beginning. Indeed, the

Fig. 20. Mozart, "Confutatis," the word "benedictis" (measures 19–25).

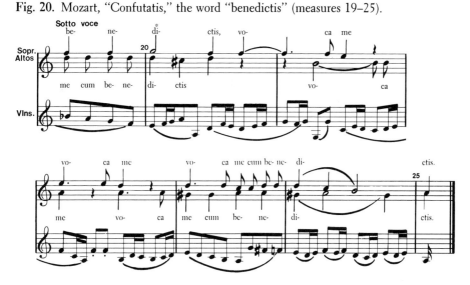

Fig. 21. Mozart, "Confutatis," soprano voice line of the concluding section (measures 26–39).

Fig. 22. Mozart, "Confutatis," the bass line, measures 14–16.

long chromatic descent of the upper voice in this second half of the movement completes the descent already begun with the word "benedictis." Taken together, the paired descents fill an entire octave in the sopranos (see Figure 23), from F^5 down to F^4 (and on into the following movement, the "Lachrymosa"; but that is another story).

The long, twisting chromatic descent in line 2 is a *tour de force:* its hushed, massed choral presentation, exchanging harmonies back and forth with a wind-instrument choir dominated by basset horns (a sound Mozart invented especially for his last works, not to be found anywhere else in music), ranks among the most unusual, somber sonic marvels of the eighteenth century. Indeed, the sinking line of uncertain destination and its guise in subtly shifting colors anticipate with startling prescience the sonic world of late-nineteenth- and twentieth-century music.

Fig. 23. Mozart, "Confutatis," the soprano descent, measures 19–39.

cum be-　ne-　di-　ctis, vo-　　ca me . . .

O-　ro　sup-plex . . .

ge- re　cu- ram me- i　fi-　　nis!

The descending chromatic melody is also a striking instance of word painting. It twists and bends lower and lower, a body ever more "supplicant and bent." It invokes not only the bowed attitude of a person praying, but also Christ to whom the prayer is addressed. The chromatic cell from which it grows is a conventional musical symbol of the Cross and Crucifixion (as in the second Kyrie of Bach's B Minor Mass, where the notes are F$^\sharp$, G, E$^\sharp$):

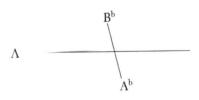

Photo 10 allows us to fix the role of line 2 in the evolving sonic design of the whole movement. The predominating features of line 2 continue the process begun in phrases 2 and 4 of line 1. This process is the progressive filtering out from the initial wide-flaring spectral complex of its higher spectral regions. First, phrases 2 and 4 ("voca me" in line 1) filters out register 7. Then, line 2 filters out register 6, and finally (in its last third) almost all of register 5. In this way, the realm of the "supplicant" descends even more into the grave regions of register 4 and below. It is this new transformation and focus on the lowest register that gives line 2 its especially somber color. With the appearance of the "supplicant," the principal spectral formation rotates around register 4 to focus in the lowest regions.

Just as the first line's paired phrases oppose dense, wide-flaring spectra ("the damned") to narrow, purified spectra ("the blessed"), so too the brighter, acute spectra of "the blessed" (and of "the damned") are now opposed to the dark, grave spectra of the "supplicant." We have now completed our view of the entire design. The piece as a whole enacts a long-range registral descent whose ultimate goal is the grave region of the "supplicant." It is from this long-range, all-transforming spectral evolution that the music of the "supplicant" derives its unique gravity and poignance. Prior to it the bright spectral regions (registers 5, 6, and 7) have been a constant presence, whether in the panoramic spectra of "the damned" or in the purified spectra of "the blessed." Only progressively and then conclusively at the close of line 2 are the higher, brighter spectral regions definitively withdrawn.

As we have already seen, the flaring spectra of the piece's first and third phrases are formed and intensified by the high formant elements of the repeated [i] vowels of the sung text. Likewise, in line 2 we now see that the grave spectra are formed and intensified by repeated [o] and [u] vowels. These grave vowels are especially prominent at the beginnings of each line in the second stanza of the text: "oro supplex . . ."; "cor contritum . . ." In his setting, Mozart takes special care to isolate these linear beginnings in the bass voices first, and then afterward to restate them in the full choral texture—both steps, isolation and repetition, emphasizing the grave color of these textual vowels.

So we find, as always, that several of music's domains—textual setting, melody and harmony, spectrum and register—combine to give the second half of the "Confutatis" its intensity and significance. Although the music of "the damned" and "the blessed" sets the spectral frame, the ultimate goal of the piece's motion and sonic transformations is the praying "I" ("mei finis"), set in the gravest colors of the piece.[2]

It is noteworthy, however, that line 2, while retaining its predominantly grave spectral coloration, at certain moments evokes the earlier music, particularly that of "the damned." This evocation occurs in two parameters. At several moments the high strings very softly rise, and then fall, through the higher spectral regions (registers 5 and 6) associated with the earlier music of the piece (see Figure 24). In a subtle way, the repeated sixteenth-note string rhythm recalls the original rhythm of "the damned" (see Figure 25). In

Fig. 24. Mozart, "Confutatis," excerpt from measures 25–26.

Fig. 25. Mozart, "Confutatis," rhythmic module from the beginning and concluding sections.

Photo 10, throughout the first half of line 2 faint traces of these spectral evocations can be seen. As line 2 continues, the traces recede and finally disappear. At the end the "supplicant" is left with only the lowest spectral regions sounding—the "ashes," rhythmically, melodically, and spectrally, of the earlier "searing flames."

It is clear that the structure of the movement, in its most physical and subtle manifestations, serves deep expressive purposes. In the light of earlier music theory it might seem that the chromatic melody quoted above, or the chains of descending suspensions, would epitomize the expressive force of this music. I believe we can now see that however powerful these events are (and musically they are very powerful), they still remain but the local, detailed, micro level of a descending motion which at the spectral, registral, macro level truly shapes and colors the entire piece from its flaring first attack to its profoundly grave last sonic trace.[3]

PHOTO 11

HECTOR BERLIOZ: TE DEUM, "TIBI OMNES ANGELI" (EXCERPT)

Performed by the London Symphony Orchestra and Chorus, and the Wadsworth School Boys' Choir: Colin Davis, conductor

Duration: 3 minutes 18 seconds

Tibi omnes angeli;	To Thee all angels,
Tibi coeli et potestates;	to Thee the heavens and all the powers,
Tibi cherubim et seraphim	to Thee cherubim and seraphim
incessabili voce proclamant:	continually do cry:
Sanctus, Sanctus, Sanctus:	Holy, Holy, Holy
Deus Sabaoth!	Lord God of Sabaoth,
Pleni sunt coeli et terra	Heaven and Earth are full
majestatis gloriae tuae . . .	of the majesty of Thy glory . . .

Compared with the "Confutatis" of Mozart's Requiem, this long excerpt from the second movement of Berlioz's Te Deum reveals another way of unfolding intense sonic and musical contrast on the largest scale. If we observe the beginning and end of Photo 11, we see that between these poles the greatest spectral distances are traversed and the greatest sonic contrasts created. As we observe the progress from one end to the other, however, we cannot fail to be struck by the gradual evolutionary course of the spectral transformation. It is as if a great space is ever more densely filled. Since even today Berlioz is a controversial (we might even say unknown) composer, and in no way more so than with respect to the structural methods of his music, it is astonishing to see so vividly realized the grand, seemingly inevitable sonic logic of his compositional design. Sharp, impressive local contrasts and oppositions are not lacking; but however many and however striking the local contrasts are, they are still absorbed into the overriding design of which they form the incidental details and subsidiary parts.

The hymn "Tibi omnes angeli" ("To Thee all angels") of the Te Deum acts like the Sanctus of a Mass. The text moves toward the repeated

"Sanctus, Sanctus, Sanctus" ("Holy, Holy, Holy") of the fifth line. Berlioz has designed this movement as a triptych of three choral-orchestral panels. Each panel begins with the incantation "Tibi . . ." ("To Thee . . ."), and moves to a climax on the repeated word "Sanctus" and the text that follows it. Each panel of the triptych is framed by an organ introduction and conclusion. Photo 11 shows the organ introduction and the first of the three principal choral-orchestral panels.

The canonic organ introduction, line 1 of Photo 11, begins and ends with spectra concentrated in registers 3 and 4 (see Figure 26). By comparison with what follows, we see that the spectra of this organ introduction are sparse, sustained, and grave. This is a result not only of the rhythms and notes, concentrated in registers 3 and 4, played by the organ. It is also a result of Berlioz's instruction that the organist use *flauti* (flute) registration. From the varied sonic repertoire of the organ, Berlioz has chosen the specific spectral color that most limits the sound to the notated fundamental pitches. In registers 3 and 4 flute registration gives a sound that is spectrally limited, dull, and flute-like. Only for a moment is the middle of line 1, as the upper organ line ascends through register 5 toward register 6, is there a momentary foreshadowing of the brighter registers and sonic qualities that, for the most part, are missing here in the introduction.

The organ introduction closes with the darkest and gravest of its sounds—an ending that emphasizes its spectral character as a choir of somber, deep-hued "flutes" (end of line 1). It is immediately followed by a sound of entirely opposing spectral placement and sonic character. This next spectrum, acute and vibrant, is wholly concentrated in registers 5, 6, and 7 and is produced by high woodwinds (flutes, oboes, clarinets) and high women's voices (see Figure 27). The women's voices enter with the repeated word "Tibi," with its four resoundings of the vowel [i]. The high woodwinds and women's voices on [i] together activate spectral regions in registers 6 and 7 previously lacking in the organ introduction. These sounds are bright, and alive with the vibrato of flute and voices. The vibrato appears in Photo 11 as the infinitesimal waverings of the spectral strands. Compared with the rigidity of the foregoing organ sounds, the vibrato waverings add a second level of contrast, and of vitalizing sonic life.

In the beginning of the "Tibi omnes angeli" we find that the total spectral range is partitioned into two opposing realms. There is the organ in flute registration, covering registers 2–4; and the high women's voices and woodwinds, covering registers 5–7. Throughout the first half of line 2 (of Photo 11) the two sonic realms, grave and acute, alternate in opposition. (See the organ interpolations after the words "angeli" and "potestates.") This partitioning recurs as the voices dwell on the word "Tibi," or on others that approach or match its sonic and semantic contents: "*angeli*" (angels), "*coeli*" (heavens), "cherubim," and "seraphim." The brightest possible vowel sounds of Latin and a text of God, heaven, and angels are all focused in the acute spectral regions.

At the end of line 2 the words of the text lead into a new verbal and

Photo 11. Berlioz, Te Deum, "Tibi omnes angeli."

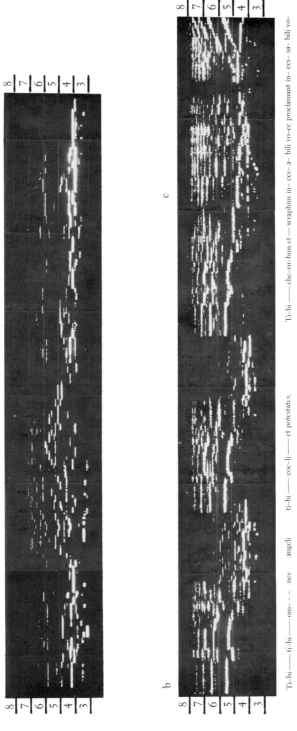

Photo 11. (continued)

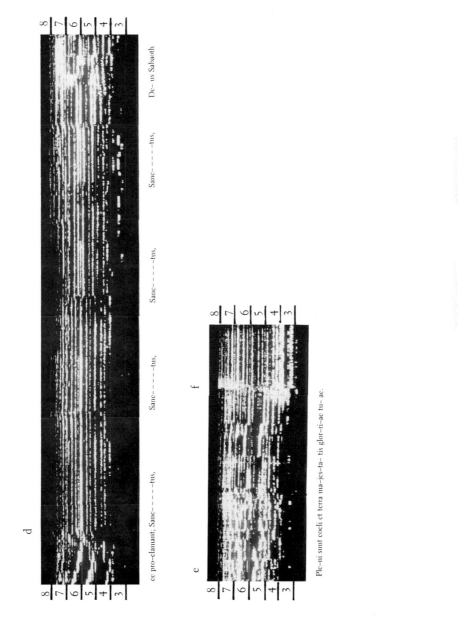

83   LARGE MIXED ENSEMBLES

Fig. 26. Berlioz, "Tibi omnes angeli," beginning.

Fig. 27. Berlioz, "Tibi omnes angeli," entrance of the soprano voices and woodwinds (measures 17–18).

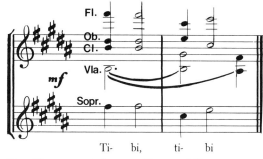

Ti-   bi,   ti-   bi

musical quality. The repeated text, "incessabili voce proclamant," ends by repeating the vowels [o] and [a]. As we have seen in many earlier examples, these vowels introduce a darker vowel quality, caused by the location of their spectral formant resonances in registers 4–5, opposed to the register 7 resonance of the previously stressed [i]. With this change of vowel quality, the women's melodic voice line descends from register 5 into register 4. There it is joined by a new set of lower orchestral instruments, principally French horns and cellos, which activate registers 3 and 4. Opposed to the earlier narrow bands of grave and acute focus is a new, wider band of resonance, generated jointly by lower women's voices and lower vowel spectral resonance. These vocal qualities are each intensified by matching orchestral instrumentation.

Suddenly there appears, in line 3 of Photo 11, one of the most memorable sounds of this Te Deum: the flickering color achieved with the long-sustained and repeated word "Sanctus." The photo's change of texture is striking. Instead of the sustained spectral strands, rigid or wavering, of the previous lines, the entire texture of line 3 is permeated by fragmentary spectral dots, a distinctive sonic pointillism. The orchestral instrumentation is unusual. In the woodwinds, arpeggio patterns run constantly and rapidly over the same groups of notes, simultaneously ascending and descending. Though all of the details are in flux, the total texture remains static.

With the appearance of the word "Sanctus" we can fully define the unfolding structural process of the excerpt. The spectral elements have become more active in both space and time. As the spectral space fills, so too is the time ever more actively subdivided and filled in. The opening out, partitioning, and combining of spectral space regions have played an important role in this process, as has the progression from rigid, to wavering, to speckled spectral strands—spectral strands ever more rapidly attacked and activated in time.

The way has thus systematically been prepared for the final burst of space-filling and space-activating sounds in line 4 that completes the section with the words: "Pleni sunt coeli et terra / majestatis gloriae tuae" ("Heaven and Earth are full / of the majesty of Thy glory"). The sonic culmination of the section is the last syllable of line 4, "tu-*ae*." There the bass drum activates the lowest extremity, register 2, while four or five pairs (Berlioz's specification) of vibrating cymbals activate the highest extremity, register 8. These percussion sounds join with the added boys' and men's voices and the orchestra in filling the entire sonic range, registers 2–8, with intense spectral activity and resonance.

Opposed to the soft, sustained, limited low-register spectral strands of the first organ sounds of this piece is this loud, noise- and attack-filled, densely packed, register-sweeping burst of choral, orchestral, and percussive sound at its end. All of the momentary oppositions of the section have prepared the way for this crowning, all-embracing opposition of sonic qualities which frames the structure. Although much attention has been devoted to the size of the forces Berlioz sometimes brings into play, less attention has been devoted to the extraordinary scope of sonic contrast that he achieves by this method. The strength of the piece derives from Berlioz's ability to activate gradually—in retrospect almost imperceptibly—the space and time of this hymn so that at its culmination both parameters are active and alive. Berlioz was a pioneer in the presentation and ordering of this range of sonic oppositions. Photo 11 shows that he realizes this enormous sonic structure with a profoundly classical logic.[4]

PHOTO 12
CLAUDE DEBUSSY: "NUAGES"
Performed by the Czech Philharmonic Orchestra: Jean Fournet, conductor
Duration: 7 minutes 50 seconds

Debussy's orchestral Nocturnes, especially the first, "Nuages" ("Clouds"), have played a crucial role in the history of tone color composition and analysis. Fortunately, we have an account in words and in sketches of Debussy's struggles (the term seems fully justified) throughout the 1890s to compose these luminous pieces.

As early as 1892 he wrote that the "three scenes of Dusk" were "almost finished." Reversing the academic cliché that a work is first "composed" and then "orchestrated," he wrote: "The orchestration being entirely completed, it is no more than a question of composition."[5] Ironic or not, Debussy's reversal points up the structural significance that orchestral color would assume from then on in his music.

In 1892, however, neither orchestration nor composition of "Nuages"

Photo 12. Debussy, "Nuages."

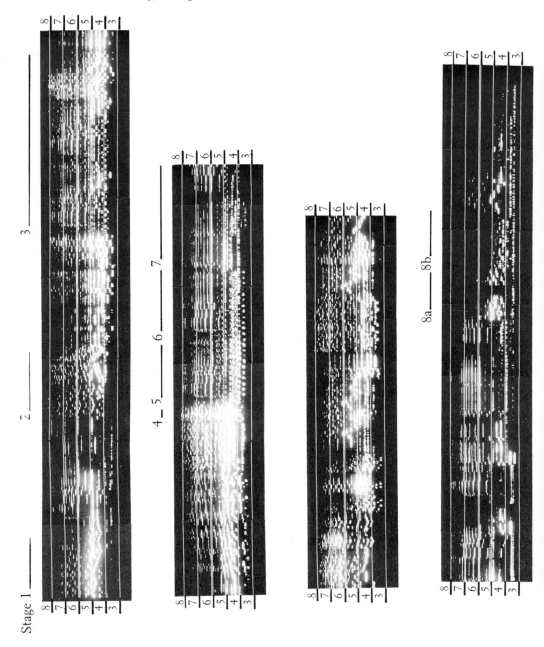

was anywhere near its ultimate form. Two years later, Debussy wrote to the violinist Eugène Ysaye about the projected work, now conceived as a concerto for violin and orchestral strings: the piece "is on the whole an exploration of the different arrangements that a single color can give—as, for example, in painting, a study in gray."[6] A study in visual color had become a metaphor for "Nuages." It remained so in 1900, when he wrote a program note for the completed orchestral work: "It is not a question of the usual form of nocturne, but rather of the impressions and special lights that the work evokes. 'Nuages' is the unchanging face of the sky with the slow, solemn motion of clouds, ending in a gray anguish softly shaded with white."[7]

Orchestration first; different arrangements of a single color; a study in gray; not the usual form; special lights; a gray anguish . . . Like the music itself, the words offer a set of stimulating, challenging clues. In 1976 Pozzi Escot and I suggested a new approach to the structural comprehension of "Nuages." In *Sonic Design* we presented a detailed study, perhaps the first anywhere, of the coordination of spectral elements and pitch motion in a musical work. We suggested that in "Nuages" these features work together to create tone color contexts and their sonic similarities, transformations, and oppositions:

> The sonic design results, then, from precise coordination of the movement of fundamental pitches with transformations of instrumental spectra and dynamics. Other possible choices of instrumental sound and dynamics would destroy this spectral design. "Nuages" forms a great motion of musical space and color. From the spatially limited, spectrally pure, noiseless and beatless tone color of the beginning, the motion proceeds to wide, rich spectra which then descend and diminish. By the end of the piece, constant attack noise and interference almost annihilate the fundamental pitches. The design begins with the first clear note of the clarinets and bassoons and ends with the last noise-drenched low B of pizzicati strings and tremolo timpani.[8]

The spectral basis of the analysis in *Sonic Design* was derived not from direct spectrum analysis but from readings in the analytical literature of spectrum analysis of single instruments. On the basis of those readings, estimates were made of the spectral formations of a few samples from crucial passages in "Nuages." At that time the complete spectral analysis of an entire orchestral work was still a distant dream. Now we can compare those estimates, and the conclusions drawn from them, with the thorough spectral analysis of every moment of "Nuages." Much of what necessarily was informed speculation in *Sonic Design* is now demonstrable fact.

The space-color transformations of "Nuages" unfold in three phases, comprising eight different stages (see Stages 1–8b in Photo 12, and Details *a–i*). *Phase I (Stage 1)* shows a relatively narrow, sparse spectral distribution focused in registers 4 and 5 (see Detail *a*). *Phase II (Stages 2–4)* displays outward spectral expansion, both ascending and descending, and increasing spectral density—finally completely filling the piece's widest spectral expanse, registers 3–8 (see Details *b–d*). *Phase III (Stages 5–8b)* is characterized by a spectral descent and decreasing spectral density, leading to a sparse,

Photo 12, Details a–j.

a
Stage 1 (measure 1)

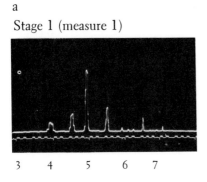

3   4   5   6   7

b
Stage 2 (measure 11)

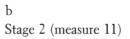
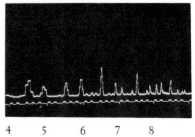

4   5   6   7   8

c
Stage 3 (measure 29)

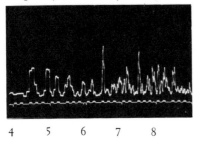

4   5   6   7   8

d
Stage 4 (measure 42)

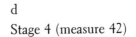
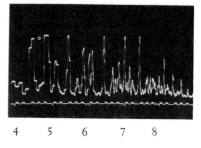

4   5   6   7   8

e
Stage 5 (measure 43)

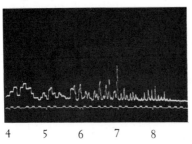

4   5   6   7   8

f
Stage 6 (measure 49)

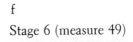
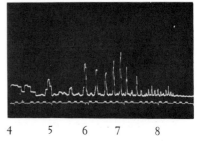

4   5   6   7   8

g
Stage 7 (measure 51)

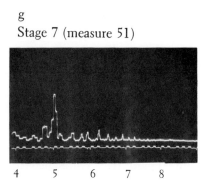

4   5   6   7   8

h
Stage 8a (measure 94)

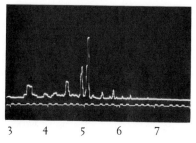

3   4   5   6   7

i
Stage 8b (measure 97)

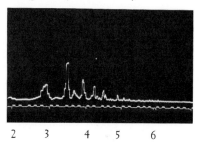

2   3   4   5   6

j
Measure 5:
English horn F^4 (plus bassoons
G^3, B^3; and clarinets G^4, B^4)

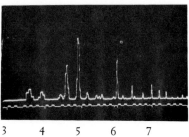

3   4   5   6   7

Fig. 28. Debussy, "Nuages," beginning (Phase I, Stage 1).

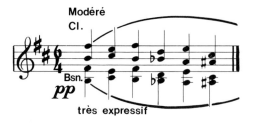

narrow distribution concentrated in the piece's lowest registers, registers 2–4 (see Details *e–i*).

From the spectral center (Phase I), the first set of transformations (Phase II) is *expansive*, both in spectral range and spectral density. Then the second set of transformations (Phase III) is simultaneously spectrally *diminishing* (in range and density) and *descending*. These three phases unfold in lines 1, 2, and 4 of Photo 12. Line 3 contains an episodic interruption that will be discussed below; by momentarily blocking it from view, the reader can see that line 4 is the direct continuation of line 2.

All of the later spectral transformations of "Nuages" are played off against the initial spectrum presented in Phase I (see Figure 28). Its sparse, centered spectrum, with its few principal partials located in registers 4 and 5, exactly in the middle of the human audible range, is clearly presented in Detail *a*. Like the sustained organ sounds of the introduction of Berlioz's "Tibi omnes angeli," these sustained clarinet-bassoon sounds also lack "internal incidents." Their regular and "solemn" (Debussy's word) flow is unbroken by attack sounds, internal waverings, interruptions, or interference. Space and time are left open, to be filled by the transformations throughout Phases II and III. Each of the coming transformations displays the regular quarter-note motion of Phase I in a newly shaded spectral coloration.[9]

The transformations of Phase II (Stages 2–4) are expansive, both in spectral range and spectral density. These spectral expansions are vividly revealed in Details *b–d*. (Note that these details add an additional upward octave, register 8, to the registers shown in Detail *a* and in Photo 12.) This expansive process leads to the spectral climax of the piece in Stage 4, where six full registers (3–8) are packed with intense spectral activity.

Close examination of the spectral strands of Stages 2–4 also reveals that they begin to display internal incidents. Minute waverings of string vibrato begin to ruffle the previously straight spectral strands. Similarly, the dense packing of space causes acoustic beats which unsettle the previously smooth sonic surface. Again like Berlioz's "Tibi omnes angeli," a parallel transformation affects both musical space and musical time. Both become more densely packed and active.

Although the dense packing of musical space is reversed after the spectral climax in Stage 4, the active packing of musical time will continue to intensify to the very end of "Nuages." Stage 4 begins a process of spectral *decrease* and *descent* which is completed only at the end of the movement.

Throughout Stages 5, 6, 7, 8a, and 8b we see the gradual disappearance of spectral elements in registers 8, 7, 6, and 5 (Details e–i). As the spectral activity diminishes in density and quantity, it shifts its focus to ever lower, darker regions. At the same time, the speckled spectral elements caused by the strings' pizzicato and tremolo and by timpani rolls all reveal ever-finer subdivisions of musical time (Photo 12, Stages 5–8b). As Photo 12 shows, the low-register focus and speckled activity of the rolling timpani and pizzicati strings give the ending a dark spectral focus and a noise-drenched texture unlike anything yet heard in the piece. Still, it is the inevitable outcome and goal of the entire process of transformation that has unfolded from the piece's beginning.

Why does line 3 interrupt the continuous descent from line 2 to line 4? The interruption serves several different purposes, the most important of which is to dramatize the spectral descent to the conclusion. It does this by interrupting the darkening spectral colors with an entire line that recalls, using extremely subtle gestures, the brightest and highest spectral colors of the earlier stages of the movement. At the start of line 3 the notes repeat those of the piece's beginning, but are given a new instrumentation, in oboes and solo viola (unmuted), which reactivates the highest spectral regions (throughout registers 6 and 7). The passage echoes, at one and the same moment, two separate earlier gestures: the notes of the beginning, and the spectral quality of the climactic Stages 3 and 4.

In the recurrence of this music at the beginning of lines 1 and 3 we see the power of spectral transformation and of changing context. The similar music plays two entirely different roles. Had "Nuages" begun with the instrumentation and spectrum of line 3 (as it might have), no space would have remained open for the upward spectral transformations of Phase II. There would have been no opposition of the centered, limited, unwavering sine-tone-like spectra of Stage 1 to the widely spread, dense, intense, high-register spectra of Stages 3–4. Oboes and unmuted strings with their high-spectrum intensity and their wavering vibrato must be saved for later. Beginning with clarinets and bassoons, and then gradually adding small quanta of *muted* strings, leaves room for the increasing activation of registers 6, 7, and 8 that occurs throughout Phase II.

We can now observe a structural nicety in Debussy's design. Just as the final descent of line 4 is dramatized by a preceding episode of high-spectrum activity (line 3), so is the spectral climax of Stage 4 dramatized by a preceding episode of low-spectrum activity, at the beginning of line 2. The beginning of line 2 is the first and greatest moment of concentrated low-register focus so far in the piece, leading to a brief episode that ascends directly to the spectral climax in Stage 4. Both here and later, we find that the most intense culminations of spectral and registral color (the climax and the conclusion) are powerfully intensified by being juxtaposed with their spectral opposites, the contrasting episodes at the beginning of line 2 and in line 3.

Between the oppositions that mark its beginning, spectral climax, and ending, "Nuages" creates a flow of spectral transformations, of constantly

Fig. 29. Debussy, "Nuages," English horn motif.

changing sonic contexts. No context simply recurs. No moment is entirely like any previous moment. Similar, reminiscent gestures are transformed so that they play essentially different roles. It is no wonder that Debussy required ten years to arrive at this richness and clarity.

The process of sonic transformation is especially striking as it affects the one element, seemingly fixed and unchanging, around which the whole movement revolves. This is the recurring, almost obsessive motif of the solo English horn (see Figure 29). The English horn spectrum is a complex one, especially rich in register 6 (see Detail *j*). When it first appears at the close of Stage 1, it foreshadows the enrichment of the highest spectral registers that will appear in the transformations of Phase II. Then in Phase III (Stages 5–7) the English horn recurs as a last fading echo of sonic qualities that are gradually disappearing as the spectral environment turns increasingly dark.

The English horn provides a fixed axis in mid-space and a constant sonic reference around which the color transformations of the entire movement turn.[10] Indeed, all of the sonic transformations of "Nuages" might be viewed as ways of reflecting and bringing forward various features—dark or bright, high or low—of its complex spectrum, as it appears in the changing lights of its many different sonic environments.

As Debussy himself said, these are "different arrangements" of a "single color": clouds, revealing many spectra, many grays.[11]

PHOTO 13
ALBAN BERG: WOZZECK, ACT III, SCENE 2, MEASURES 109–121
Performed by the Paris Opera Orchestra; Pierre Boulez, conductor
Duration: 27 seconds

Is a single note merely a note alone, or is it more than that? The question is implicit on every page of this book. Nowhere is it raised more urgently than at the climax of *Wozzeck's* murder scene, which dwells on a single note, B, for almost a half minute.

An "invention on one note" is Berg's description of this scene. He reports that he chose the note B[3] for this climactic moment because it is "the only note of the entire scale which belongs to *all* the instruments of the orchestra; it starts in the softest pianissimo possible in the muted French horn and increases its sonority through gradually louder orchestral entries up to the most powerful outburst."[12] (See Table 1.) What is striking about the image of this climactic passage in Photo 13 is the constancy of its transformation. The sonic event that the photo records is neither simple nor static. It shows

Table 1. Instrumental entrances in *Wozzeck*, Act III, Scene 2.

WINDS	STRINGS
1 French horn, muted	
	Solo violin, muted
1 Bass clarinet	
	All violins I
4 Clarinets	
3 French horns	Solo viola
	Solo cello
4 Oboes	
	All violins II
4 Trumpets	
3 Bassoons and tuba	
4 Trombones	All violas
	All cellos
	All double basses

Note: All instruments enter *pppp* and gradually crescendo to their greatest dynamic power.

an unfolding sonic evolution whose elements are varied, opposed, and mixed in new ways, even as the lowest fundamental note remains (for the most part) the constant B^3. Photo 13 is one of the most arresting of all the spectrum photos, and its visual drama is directly related to its sonic drama.

The almost inaudible B^3 of the muted French horn begins with a spectrum reduced to the absolute minimum: a pure B^3 fundamental. In Photos 11 and 12 we saw complex structures evolve from very sparse, limited spectral beginnings. Such a spectral beginning allows for the growth of later developments and transformations. At the beginning of this climactic passage, Berg has carried spectral reduction to its ultimate. He presents the dynamic and spectral minimum, to which the dynamic and spectral maxima at the ends of each of the two sonic phrases will be shatteringly opposed.

The first phrase proceeds through two stages of sonic transformation (Photo 13, first half). In the first stage, the pitched instruments of the orchestra enter on the note B^3, a pure, sine-tone-like fundamental. As each instrument enters and gradually crescendos from as soft as possible to as loud as possible, the harmonic spectrum of B^3 increases in range and complexity. From the single partial of its beginning, the harmonic spectrum expands to eighteen partials covering registers 4, 5, 6, and 7.

It is not mere changing loudness, or changing masses of instruments, that causes the growth of this harmonic spectrum; the choice and order of appearance of the instruments are, as well, responsible for the spectral curve. B^3 is initially sounded by instruments whose spectrum, at *pppp*, is almost entirely fundamental: muted French horn, muted solo violin, and solo bass clarinet. Only as the harmonic spectrum evolves toward its peak do such

Photo 13. Alban Berg, *Wozzeck,* Act III, Scene 2.

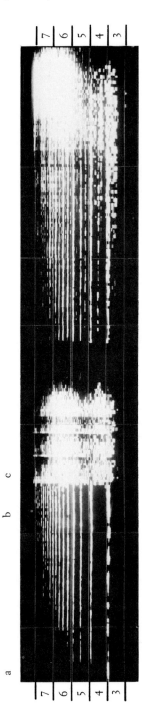

spectrally rich instruments as oboes, trumpets, and trombones appear. The transformation from spectral nothingness to spectral richness, as from maximal softness to maximal loudness, is a direct consequence of this instrumental ordering.

At its apex, the five-octave space opened up by the growing harmonic spectrum on B^3 is abruptly filled in by a series of violent rhythmic attacks on the bass drum. The bass drum densely packs registers 3–7 with spectral elements. Consequently, the most opposing sonorities—the almost inaudible, pure spectrum of the muted French horn and the shattering booms of the bass drum—have been organically connected by the spectral-registral ascent of the harmonic spectrum.

The second phrase is not a mere echo of the first, although it, too, enacts both a dynamic crescendo and a spectral ascent (see Photo 13, second half). In the second phrase both of these transformational features, the crescendo and the ascent, are primarily created by the percussion instruments of the orchestra. This phrase adds to the wind and string instruments of the first phrase a battery of rolling, crescendoing percussion: snare drum, timpani, cymbals, and tam-tams (gongs). In Photo 13 we can see, in the interstices between the harmonic spectral elements of the note B, the mounting spectral elements of this constant percussion crescendo. They ascend from the lowest register, register 3, filling the cracks of the spectral space. At the end, the percussion spectrum concentrates in the highest registers—6, 7, and upward. This percussive noise-band ascent is at once the analog and the opposite of the smooth harmonic ascent of the first phrase. It is analogous in its steadily rising intensification through registers 3–7; it is opposing in its clotted noise-band spectral density and its speckled, constant-attack pattern. The second phrase emerges as an original, fascinating sonic variant of the first.

The entire passage, having begun purely and almost inaudibly, ends with an overwhelming burst of noise resonance in the highest audible regions, stretching upward from registers 6–8. It is obvious that the ending thus opposes the beginning. It is perhaps less obvious (but equally graphic in Photo 13) that the percussion ending of phrase 2 is also precisely opposed to the percussion ending of phrase 1. The bass drum spectra at the end of phrase 1 curve down to their original low registers, and then decay into silence (see Photo 13, middle). In contrast, the closing burst of snare drum, cymbal, and tam-tam resonance, *fff*, sizzles up into the highest sonic regions—and then onward into the raucous beginning of the next scene. To the spectral descent and decay of the end of the first phrase, the end of the second phrase opposes spectral ascent and extreme sonic intensification.

Like the murder scene, this climactic passage reaches the ultimate in human limits, extending from the threshold of audibility to the threshold of pain. Far from being a simple uniform event—a single, static note, B—it is a highly shaped musical complex. But what shape? A complex of what? As is true of the other formations we have observed in this book, its shaping is spectral and sonic. It is defined by moments of sonic, spectral opposition and their connections. Here, as elsewhere, the array of sonic oppositions is unexpectedly rich. There is opposition of the purest, simplest spectrum to complex spectra; the opposition of harmonic spectra to noise spectra; the opposition of low registers to high; of narrow spectra to wide; of ascending to descending spectral contours; of space filling to space emptying (reaching the ultimate decay, silence); of soft to loud; of no attack to constant, speckled attack. The shaping power of these oppositions, bringing one another into being, forms this striking climactic passage and produces "an irresistible effect": "In every performance of *Wozzeck* . . . [it] literally drags the audience from their seats."[13]

It is a spectral, sonic invention on one note.[14]

PHOTO 14
EDGARD VARÈSE: HYPERPRISM

Performed by the Paris Instrumental Ensemble for Contemporary Music; Konstantin Simonovitch, conductor

Duration: 4 minutes 45 seconds

"On the threshold of beauty, science and art collaborate."[15] In this way, Varèse enunciated his ideal of science and art working together. During the 1920s and 1930s he and Harvey Fletcher, for many years director of research at Bell Laboratories, pioneered in work uniting musical composition and sonic science. As one result of this effort, Varèse predicted the development of a seismographic notation of music.[16] The photographic analyses in this book go far toward realizing his vision.

Photo 14 vividly pictures the "movement of sound masses" evoked by Varèse. We clearly see the opacities and rarefactions, differentiations and collisions which he spoke of so often.[17]

Each line of the photo can be regarded as one face of a three-sided prism, each face reflecting and reproducing the structure of the other faces. The design of each line consists of massive sonorities at both ends, surrounding an area of sonic rarefaction. At the midpoint of each line, the rarefaction is bisected by a brief spectral eruption. Consequently, the crystalline design displays multiple reflections. Each line reflects its own structure, symmetrically, around an axial midpoint; and each line reflects, as well, the similar structure of the other lines.

Opacities and *rarefactions:* the words themselves suggest the play of densities in opposition. In *Hyperprism,* oppositions of density take at least two different forms: *compact/diffuse* and *sparse/rich.* (These terms will be discussed in detail in Part II. We have seen important sparse/rich oppositions in Photos 2 and 7). The opposition compact/diffuse refers to the relative density of the individual spectral elements. Such elements can be narrow spectral strands, encountered most notably in harmonic spectra (compact), or they can be the wider spectral bands characteristic of noises and some percussion sounds (diffuse). For *Hyperprism,* Varèse created an instrumental ensemble of nine wind instruments arrayed against sixteen percussion instruments played by six players. The ensemble makes available a wide variety of compact and diffuse sounds and can express the whole range of spectral phenomena embraced by this opposition.

The sectional designs of *Hyperprism* express this opposition as well. The areas of rarefaction are dominated again and again by the compact spectral strands of wind instruments. For example, see the flute solo at *i* in the photo (measures 19–23); or the ensemble of wind instruments at *m* (measures 39–42). These central rarefied, compact textures are surrounded at the extremities of each line by the opaque, diffuse spectral bands of the percussion.

The eruptions that mark the exact center of each line are created, in lines 1 and 3, by the collision of the opposing instrumental bodies (winds/percussion) and sonic qualities (compact/diffuse). Varèse's description of the collision of sound masses is one of the most evocative in all his writings: "The movement of sound masses will be clearly perceived in my work, taking the place of linear counterpoint. When these sound masses collide, the phenomenon of penetration or repulsion will seem to occur . . . The role of color or *timbre* would be completely changed from being incidental, anecdotal, sensual, or picturesque; it would become an agent of delineation, like the different colors on a map separating different areas, and an integral part of form."[18]

In addition to the density of the *individual* spectral elements, there is also the relative density of the *total* spectral formation at any moment, sparse or rich. The examples of sonic rarefaction just cited (*i* and *m*) are at the same time compact (narrow spectral strands) and sparse (relatively few of them).

Where both density features combine to thin out the spectrum, the rarefaction is greatly intensified by the combination of sparse and compact elements; but density features need not always reinforce one another. In *Hyperprism* Varèse combines, and recombines, various sonic qualities in diverse ways, engendering new collisions. An example is the percussion progression at the very beginning:

a crashed cymbals
  struck tam-tam
  struck and rolled bass drum (loud)

b rolled and struck bass drum (soft)
  lion's roar (string drum) crescendo

All of these sounds create diffuse spectral bands. However, individually and in combination they display a variety of spectral widths. The cymbals, tam-tam, and loud bass drum light up very broad spectral bands. Indeed, at their maximum, they cover virtually all of the audible spectrum (see *a* in the photo). They are rich as well as diffuse. In contrast, the soft bass drum and the lion's roar, even at its maximum, cover only the lower half of the spectrum, registers 2–5 (see *b*), and can best be described as sparse. Thus, diffuse sounds are shown to be either rich or sparse, depending on spectral width. Recognizing these sonic possibilities, Varèse joins and orders these percussion sounds at the beginning of *Hyperprism* so that they progress from diffuse and rich (*a*) to diffuse and sparse (*b*). This is only the first

Photo 14. Edgard Varèse, *Hyperprism*.

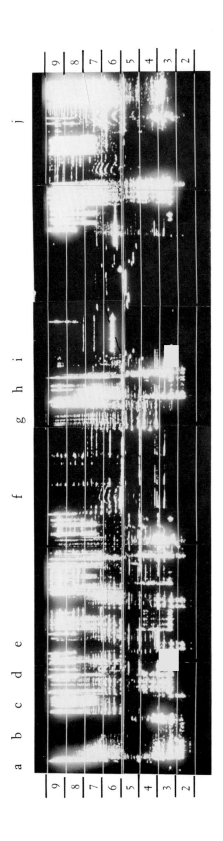

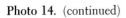

Photo 14. (continued)

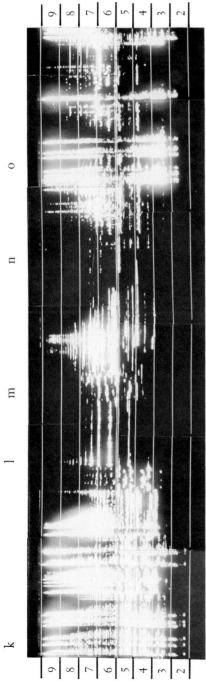

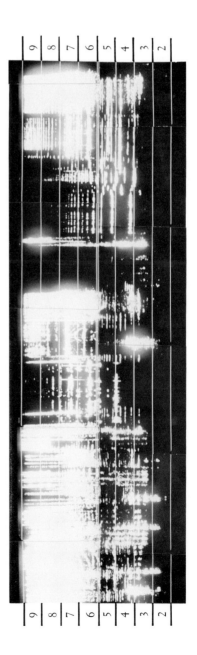

Fig. 30. Varèse, *Hyperprism*, the succession of density qualities.

a	b	c	(f, i)
diffuse	diffuse	compact	(compact)
rich	sparse	rich	(sparse)
meas. 0	meas. 1	meas. 1	(mm. 12, 20)

stage of a more extended progression of related sonic transformations.

Compact spectra, while frequently sparse, can also on occasion be rich. Varèse shows this with the next sound in the piece (*c* in the photo): the muted trombone, *ff*, which immediately follows the lion's roar and which richly kindles the entire high spectral region, registers 4–9. Varèse here returns to the initial rich spectrum—not with the original diffuse percussion, but with a variant composed of the compact muted trombone spectrum.

It is exciting to find revealed, in this way, the structural relationships and progression of the beginning of *Hyperprism*. In the first percussion sounds the entire spectral range is rapidly activated. That complete spectrum is then broken down, as by a prism, into its components—elements that are recombined in different ways. The different density qualities offer four possibilities of combination. Three of these are used by Varèse immediately to create the initial sonic textures of *Hyperprism* (see Figure 30). The fourth combination—compact, sparse—is held in reserve to create the area of rarefaction in the middle of line 1.

Photo 14 shows how line 1 is based upon a progression from the maximum opacity and density to the minimum. The maximally dense features, diffuse and rich, are paired at *a*. The minimally dense features, compact and sparse, are paired in the rarefied midsection of the line, *f* and *i*. Between these two extremes, the pairings mix one maximally and one minimally dense feature (*b* and *c*). In this way, *b* and *c* effect a sonic transition between the extremes at the beginning and midpoint. Underlying all of line 1 is a progression from maximally to minimally dense sonorities—and, at the end, a return to the maximally dense.

At the spectral eruption that bisects line 1 we find once again the interplay of the various kinds of spectral density. At the precise moment when spectral richness erupts in the midst of sparsity, the two kinds or richness (compact and diffuse) are placed side by side. First, there is the compact richness of the winds' nine-note *f-fff* sonority, its ladder-like spectrum filling six registers, 4–9. Next to it, the percussion again flashes through the entire audible range, creating the same diffuse richness that began the piece. Then, both forms of density subside at once into utter sparsity: the varied forms of density collide and explode into near-nothingness.

Density—like *sound masses, collisions, opacities,* and *rarefactions*—is an evocative word in Varèse's vocabulary. We have only to think of his solo flute work, titled *Density 21.5*. In Photo 14 the play of spectral densities and of different qualities of spectral density clearly emerges as basic to the structure of *Hyperprism*. Density oppositions, however, are not the only crucial oppositions. The rich, range-covering percussion flash at the very beginning is filtered, or refracted, not only on the basis of density but also on the basis of spectral register.

Just as density was analyzed as the result of a pair of criteria (compactness/diffuseness; sparseness/richness), so too is there a pair (at least) of criteria for spatial placement. These are the criteria of "height," grave/acute; and of "width," wide/narrow (see the discussion in Part II). With these terms, we can spatially characterize the marvelously rapid set of percussion transformations that begins *Hyperprism*: from *a*—acute and wide, with cymbals and tam-tam *fff*—the piece moves to *b*, which is grave and narrow, and marked by a bass drum roll diminuendo to *p*, muted.

What a special moment *b* turns out to be! We have already observed the density change as the initial percussion flash falls away to the lowest registers: richness becomes sparseness. At the same time, each of the spatial features is reversed—what was originally acute becomes grave, and what was wide becomes narrow. The acute edge of the percussion flash at *a*, caused by the brilliant attack of the cymbals, is transformed at *b* into the totally contrasting speckled rumble of the diminuendo, and then muffled, bass drum roll. Here, too, having defined the sonic extremes, we can observe how Varèse creates sonic transitions. Between the cymbal attack that begins *a* and the soft bass drum that defines *b* are two transitional stages: the successive *fff* attacks of the tam-tam and the bass drum. These transitional attacks carry the registral focus from registers 8 and 9 *down* toward registers 2 and 3, even while activating wide, dense spectral bands.

These beginning moments of percussive sound are spectrally extremely varied and suggestive, and important because all of their elements and oppositions foreshadow elements and oppositions that emerge on a larger scale in *Hyperprism*. The above-described sonic "chute" at *a-b*, where density and register dramatically fall away, is a gesture that reappears at *d* and *e* in line 1 of Photo 14. In each chute a prevailing rich, wide, acute, loud texture (*d*) abruptly drops to a contrasting sparse, narrow, grave, soft texture (*e*):

d	*e*
Muted tenor trombone ($C^{#4}$)———————→	French horns ($C^{#4}$) Muted bass trombone (D^2)
Snare drum Indian drum ————————→	Bass drum
Tambourine Triangles ————————→	Cymbals Tam-tam (large gong)
Rattles	
(*ff* prevails)	(*p* prevails)

Each instrumental family shows a transformation from acute to grave spectra between columns *d* and *e*. This is obvious in the percussion progression of triangles to tam-tam and snare drum to bass drum. But it is equally true of the progression of high to very low muted trombone ($C^{\#4}$ to D^2), and the transfer of $C^{\#4}$ from muted trombone (with its wide acute spectrum) to open French horn (with its limited grave spectrum). In all of these cases, the grave registral character of *e* is reinforced by its softer dynamic, for softer sounds typically generate fewer high spectral elements than louder ones. Gravity and softness make a natural, although not inevitable, pairing.

At *e* and thereafter, each spectral chute reenacts the gesture fore-shadowed at *b*. Consequently, the germinal gesture implanted at *b* finds its structural fulfillment throughout line 1. The fulfillment is sonic and spectral in nature, rather than melodic or harmonic. As Varèse has said, color has be-come the "agent of delineation." It is in the spatial deployments and densi-ties of spectra that the structural bonds are to be sought. Melodic and harmonic qualities are certainly not lacking in the piece; Varèse has at his dis-posal an impressive variety of means. However, the melodic and harmonic elements are folded into the spatial deployments and densities in such a way that these latter forces create many of the principal delineations and relation-ships.

Much of the foregoing structural description of *Hyperprism* has focused on the shaping of *percussion* sounds. Varèse's "entirely new magic of sound" resides, to a great extent, in exploring the design-creating potential of percus-sion sounds, alone or in combination with other instruments. Spectral analy-sis allows us to read the varied contours and densities of the initial percussion flash and its sonic developments with the same precision as any other sounds and sound combinations. It takes us out of the dark night of previous percus-sion notation and understanding, as it does out of the gray twilight of other instrumental notations. We have arrived at an equal illumination of musical sounds, regardless of their source—and of the formations that give them shape and, sometimes, their magical power.[19]

4.
Electronic and Tape Music

THE VAST potential of electronically synthesized music poses a novel challenge to composers, music theorists, and listeners. The materials on which such music can draw are seemingly infinite: all of the sounds and sound formations within the humanly audible ranges of frequency and intensity (occasionally even bursting beyond, into the inaudible or painful); every conceivable sonic duration, from the infinitesimal and imperceptible to the "eternal"; and the most diverse panoply of tone colors and attendant sound spectrum configurations, whether of language sounds, musical instrument sounds, natural sounds and noises, or sounds between or beyond these. Defining and understanding such riches are beyond the capabilities of previously existing theoretical systems and analytic processes.

In meeting this challenge, spectrum photos can fill a double function. First, they provide a notation for the content of synthesized music—a notation that clearly specifies, as no other does, the orientation, motion, duration, and spectral makeup of each element of the music. Second, spectrum photos provide an analytic base, with data and evidence, for conclusions about the sonic character and structural function of the sonorities and features that they picture.

Even here, in music partly or wholly bereft of all that previously has been the basis of musical understanding—notated pitches, metrical durations, musical instruments—we can, using spectrum photos, discern the constituent musical and sonic elements and the ways in which they are organized into structural formations. The photos and commentaries in this chapter are no doubt only the first step in this direction—precursors of a host of future refinements and improvements.

In Photo 15, of an excerpt from Milton Babbitt's *Ensembles for Synthesizer*, we can study the character and the specific interrelationships of a set of its most striking and varied sonorities—those that open the piece and define its sonic context. In Photo 16 we expand our view to take in an entire movement, "Fall" from Jean-Claude Risset's computer suite, *Little Boy*. An especially beautiful spectrum photo results from the traces of its previously invisible sonic transformations.

The concluding spectrum photo of the book illustrates *No Attack of Organic Metals*, which I wrote for organ and taped sounds. The work had its origin in the spectral qualities of its constituent sounds, which were originally analyzed laboriously by ear rather than by electronic spectral display. Photo 17 now provides a means of objectively confirming the presence of those sonic properties, and reveals connections between the mechanical or electrical sounds on tape and the sounds of the organ. The spectrum photo in this case documents directly, rather than by inference, my quest, as composer, for sonic relationships through sonic analysis and sonic resemblance or contrast. The analytic process that we have been studying has become part of the compositional process, the two joining together in the great twin spirals of musical understanding and creation.

PHOTO 15
MILTON BABBITT: ENSEMBLES FOR SYNTHESIZER, INTRODUCTION
Realized by the composer at the Columbia-Princeton Electronic Music Center
Duration: 54 seconds

A particular quality of the opening of *Ensembles for Synthesizer* is the way in which, with a few exemplary sounds lasting less than a minute, a whole sonic universe is summoned up. Exactly and concisely, the piece's beginning sketches a framework for all that follows.

The introduction is dominated by four separate sonic pillars: *a*, *b*, *c*, and *d* in Photo 15. The photo lets us see at once the symmetrical distribution in time of these sonic buttresses. Each lasts nine seconds; each is preceded by an introductory segment of approximately half that duration.

Each of the pillars is a distinctive sonic creation, with its own profile and character. These are not the off-the-shelf geometric wave forms (square waves, saw-tooth waves) of the most ubiquitous sorts of electronic "composition." Nor are they the instrument analogs ("trumpet-like," "voice-like") that are almost equally common. With their complex inner formations and interrelationships, these pillar-like complexes (each consisting of twenty or more spectral elements) exemplify the challenge that electronically synthesized sounds pose to our ability to understand and describe sonic character, likenesses, and differences. Given sonorities of such distinctiveness, it might seem that the means must already exist for their description, analysis, and understanding. However, we have already seen examples of sounds and sonic contexts of unusual power and distinction—Tibetan chanting, the Balinese *gamelan*, the orchestral sounds of "Nuages," the percussion formations of *Hyperprism*—that defeat the capacities of even the best of our traditional theories.

What, then, are the constituent elements of Babbitt's precisely synthesized sonic pillars? What are the special distinguishing characteristics of each? Taken as a sonic ensemble, what is the particular sense of their succession? How do they and their immediate surroundings manage to foreshadow the full sonic world of the *Ensembles?*

Figure 31, a somewhat simplified spectral model of the four sonic complexes, is derived from Photo 15. We can see that each of the complexes dis-

Photo 15. Milton Babbitt, *Ensembles for Synthesizer*, Introduction.

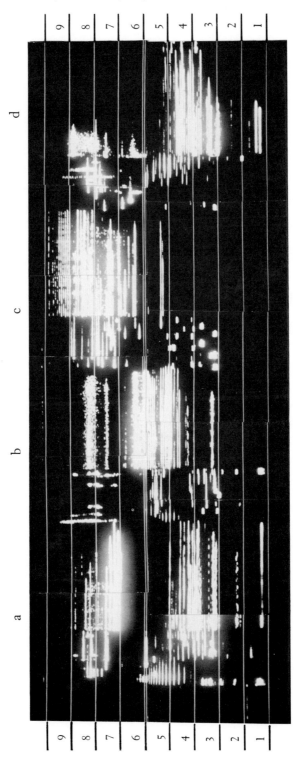

Fig. 31. Babbitt, *Ensembles for Synthesizer*, Introduction, spectral distribution in the four principal sonorities.

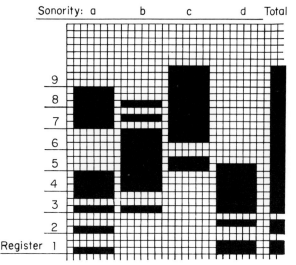

plays a unique registration—a unique selection of registral colors and a unique mixture of registral absences, presences, and saturations. The registral colors are organized so that the ensemble of sonorities progresses toward the saturated registral extremities of the last two sonorities.

On the largest scale, sonorities *a* and *b* oppose sonorities *c* and *d*: *a* and *b* are registrally mixed (acute plus grave registers), but are not focused on the registral extremities; *c* and *d* are both focused on the registral extremities (registers 6–9 in *c*, and 1–4 in *d*), but do not mix them. In *a* and *b* the mixture of registral colors, grave and acute, is achieved in two different ways. In *a* it is highlighted by the wide gap within the sonority: the almost complete emptiness of registers 5 and 6, which vividly separates the grave and acute elements and regions (registers 1–4 and 7–8) from one another. In sonority *b* the mixture of qualities is accomplished by *centering*: it intensely activates the middle registers of the context (4–6), as opposed to its sparser, briefer, and fainter acute and grave elements in registers 3, 7, and 8.

By contrast, in sonorities *c* and *d* the opposing colors grave and acute are wholly separated and intensified rather than mixed. Complex *c* focuses entirely on the acute region (registers 5–9), activating the most acute register (9) for the first time in the piece. Complex *d*, on the other hand, focuses entirely on the grave region (registers 1–4), saturating registers 3 and 4 to the greatest degree in the entire introduction.

In the largest view, then, the sonority pairs are opposed, *ab/cd*, even as the individual members of each pair are also opposed, *a/b* and *c/d*. In summary: *a* is mixed and extreme; *b* is mixed and centered; *c* is unmixed and acute; *d* is unmixed and grave. The specific registral deployment and color of each sonority is clear. So, too, is the role of each sonic complex in the unfolding succession.

Fig. 32. Transposition of the four spectral sonorities in Figure 31 to a common bass.

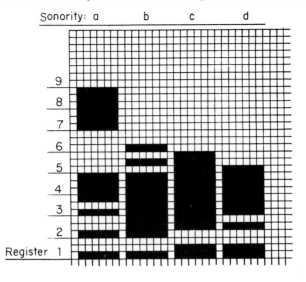

The role of sonority *b* is especially interesting. It draws the spectral focus toward the neutral center, just prior to the outward expansion to the widest extremities in *c* and *d*. This, too, heightens *c* and *d*: they not only spectrally saturate their opposing extremities, grave and acute, but arrive at those extremities by flaring out from *b* at the spectral center.

Another related property of complex *b* is revealed in Figure 32, where the complexes of Figure 31 are transposed so that they all have a common bass. We can immediately see that each sonic complex is spectrally narrower than its predecessor. It is complex *b* that begins, very intensely so, this process of spectral contraction, drawing itself in in two different senses—by reducing its total width (Figure 32), and by contracting from the spectral extremities toward its focus at the spectral center (registers 4–6; see Figure 31).

Taken together, these four introductory sonic pillars open up virtually the entire human audible range, registers 1–9 (see the "Total" column in Figure 31). They draw from that range a striking variety of mixed and pure, extreme and centered, acute and grave colorations. From its own specific spectral deployment, as well as from its systematic opposition to the other sonorities, each of the four complexes acquires its sharp profile and value just as the entire passage reveals its inevitable cohesion and sense of direction—an ever more intense spatial contraction, together with an ever more extreme concentration of color. Spatial and coloristic possibilities have been laid out for the entire piece.

Finally, Photo 15 reveals that the sonorities all display a characteristic spectral shaping in time that complements their shaping in space. Each nine-second sonority, as it approaches its conclusion, thins out. Each sonority does this in a way that retains and further intensifies its own particular sonic characteristics. For example, in *a*, characterized by a mixture of registers, elements in all of its diverse regions (registers 1, 3, 4, and 7) remain mixed to its very end, even as many spectral details disappear. In contrast in the centered sonority, *b*, it is the central registers (4 and 5) that prevail to the end, while the extremities thin out and disappear. And in the acute sonority, *c*, the most extreme acute registers (8 and 9) remain to the end.

Just as each sonority is modeled by gaps and areas of spectral saturation to achieve a specific placement and shaping in space, so too does their spectral modeling in time keep the particular sonic quality of each sonority in clear focus, even as it thins out. In other words, each sonority, as it unfolds in time, presents more, and then less, dense variants of the same registral coloration.

The entire passage reveals a sonic shape of accumulating contrasts in which each uniquely crafted and conceived sonority and each sonic transformation plays a contributing role. The details of each sonic complex are shaped in space and time in ways that reinforce the sense of the passage. They bind its elements into a coherent, self-reflecting whole which we can now perceive and model.[1]

PHOTO 16
Jean-Claude Risset: Computer suite from Little Boy, "Fall"

Realized by the composer on an IBM 7094 computer at Bell Laboratories, Murray Hill, New Jersey

Duration: 2 minutes 50 seconds

The music that Jean-Claude Risset has created for the play *Little Boy* is a special instance of the union of science, technology, and art.[2] The play itself is a psychological reconstruction of the atomic bombing of Hiroshima. In one of its sections, "Fall," the bomb's descent is associated with the human sensation of falling. Risset's music for "Fall" is pictured in Photo 16.

This music derives from an illusion of musical, or auditory, space that was discovered by the American psychologist Roger Shepard.[3] Shepard revealed that sounds can be created which seem to fall, or rise, continually and infinitely; their descent, or ascent, seems never to end. Using an IBM computer at Bell Laboratories, Risset has realized such sounds and has made the illusion of infinite descent the basis of "Fall." Scientist and composer have each made contributions to this music: it was Shepard who discovered the illusion of infinite-seeming sonic descent and the principles for realizing it; Risset shaped this illusion into the piece of music now before us.

Shepard's illusion (often called "Shepard's tones") results from partials that are overlapped in a particular way, shown by the "barber pole" spectral lines in Photo 16. As the descent progresses, the lowest partials become weaker in intensity, while higher partials creep in and become stronger. As a spectral strand descends and disappears, higher strands have already imperceptibly come to dominate the spectrum. Shepard's illusion succeeds because the multiple parallel elements confuse the registral orientation of the hearer.

In Photo 16 we see that each strand of the barber pole spectrum first ap-

Photo 16. Jean-Claude Risset, *Little Boy,* "Fall."

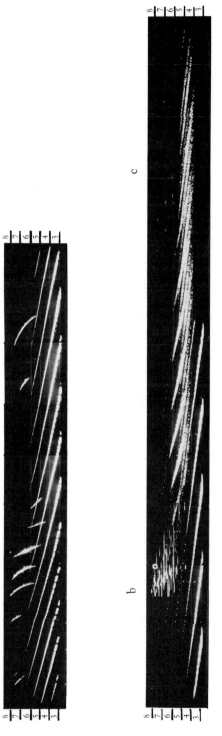

pears in register 6 and gradually drifts down through musical space. As it arrives in register 5, a new spectral strand appears at approximately the same pitch in register 6. The two strands then continue a parallel descent, until the lower one fades out, to resume in the highest register. (The viewer should disregard the apparent thickening of the strands in register 3; this is a distortion in the display. Actually, the strands are weakest at their highest and lowest extremities.) As a pair of strands continues its descent, other strands will appear in register 6. By this continuing process, the barber pole spectrum is created. A vertical cross-section of it at any point reveals a spectrum of three (at most, four) simultaneous spectral elements, at varying intensities and at approximate octave relationships. The photo shows that throughout the piece there is a continual slight flattening out and lengthening (in time) of the descents, and a corresponding slight increase in time between the entrance of new spectral strands. This variation minutely alters the octave relationships, for it means that successive spectral strands do not drift downward at quite the same rate.

Ultimately, at the end of line 2, the descending drifts cease to be single partials related by octaves (or approximate octaves) and become sonic bands, which also continue to flatten out, slow down, and merge. Photo 16 reveals this entire process—the gradual rotation of the piece on its axis, which causes the flattening out, slowing down, and ultimate centering of the elements. This happens so gradually that its stages are otherwise barely noticeable, even as it totally transforms the sonic texture in the long run (compare lines 1 and 2 of Photo 16).

The sensation of infinite falling that Risset creates, using Shepard's illusion, constitutes one constant level of "Fall." Intermittently, superimposed on this level of infinite descent, is a second, opposing level of *finite* descents. These, too, are pictured in Photo 16. Throughout line 1 the finite descents are brief trajectories in the highest registers. These trajectories initially burst out of register 7 into register 6, and then later descend further, into registers 5 and 4. Consequently, these sonic flashes fall in two different ways: while they are descending flashes, they also appear as ever-lower trajectories. More and more, they penetrate and merge into the space of the opposing infinite descents. In this way, they prefigure the centering and merging of all sonic elements in register 4 that will occur at the end of the piece.

These finite, high-register sonic flashes undergo two different kinds of transformation. The first is the spectral descent from register 7 into registers 6, 5, and 4, which unfolds through the first eight trajectories. Separate and different from these are the final two trajectories of line 1, which allude to the principal process that transforms the infinite descents: the flattening out and temporal lengthening of spectral contours. Both of the final trajectories in line 1 resemble earlier flashes. The first of them, trajectory 9, resembles the briefest flashes—trajectories 1, 3, 7, and 8. The final trajectory, 10, resembles the longer arcs—flashes 4 and 5. But both of the final trajectories are tilted more to the horizontal plane than their predecessors, so that they persist longer.

Consequently, the two levels, infinite and finite (or grave and acute) are transformed in parallel ways, undergoing independent but parallel variation. The constituent elements of both levels are progressively flattened out and lengthened in time.

Prior to the development of spectrum photos, it was very difficult to describe, and understand the kinds of spatial, temporal, and sonic—in a word, structural—relationships and transformations that are now apparent in "Fall." Photo 16 sheds light on all these elements—revealing, for example, the growing deceleration and "spacing out" of the sonic features in time. This deceleration is so gradual and so independent of previous conventions of notated musical rhythm that it has hardly been noticeable.

This is also true of the proportional formation of the movement, which likewise displays a "spacing out" of the second part (line 2) in relationship to the first part (line 1). The two parts relate in the ratio of 2:3. (Part one is 68 seconds; part two is 102 seconds; $68/102 = 0.667$.) The two parts are separated by the only break in the sonic continuity of the piece, a very short pause that occurs between the lines of the photo. It is not necessarily the exact numbers, or ratio, of the relationships of the parts that is important; rather, it is that the proportional design plays a particularly apt role in the transformational process of this piece. It enacts on the highest structural level (the relationship of the parts) that quality of spreading out and slowing down that we have found reenacted on every level. From the briefest elements and gestures—the sonic flashes and spectral strands of line 1—to the largest parts, every element flattens out and slows down.

Many of Risset's resources are new: the computers and programs that generate the sound; the electronic technology necessary for tape performance; the knowledge gained from research in sonic perception. At the same time, this striking design is equally rooted in processes of transformation and opposition that are similar, if not identical, to those of many earlier examples in this book. For example, the proportional design of "Fall" resembles that of the very first example, "Qui sedes, Domine." In the Gregorian chant, too, the resemblance goes beyond the mere similarity of numbers or ratios and resides in a similar process: the reproduction in the second part of all of the first part's structural relationships on a prolonged, more intensive scale. A similar structural plan likewise underlies Mozart's "Confutatis" (Photo 10). And the building of structures by systematically amassing opposing features, among them spectral features—which here take the forms finite/infinite, acute/grave, extreme/centered—is evident in every example in this book.

So far in "Fall" every detail and every transformation found in line 1 has played a significant role in the process of opposition building. In line 2 the paired opposition of grave and acute regions and of infinite and finite gestures continues through the unfolding transformations. The acute, finite gestures take the form not of brief flashes or trajectories, but rather of descending agglomerations of level spectral elements scattered through the acute region. We have already observed the axial tilt which thickens, flattens, and lengthens the infinite spectral strands so that they come to form the fading, dense, speckled noise bands of line 2. At both levels of line 2—at the acute, finite level and the grave, infinite level—we find the same process at work: the radical intensification of the leveling, or flattening out, of the spectral elements that has already appeared, in line 1, as the basic transformational process of the piece.

Consequently, we find in part two of "Fall" that each level—the finite, acute and the infinite, grave—inclines more and more toward the unchanging, the fixed, and the horizontal. Not only do the individual strands of the infinite level tilt more and more to the horizontal and lengthen, but they also break up, in much of line 2, into small *fixed* descending pellets of sound. As the sonic elements become increasingly fixed yet broken up, one other transformational process is set into action: the progressive falling off of loudness. Fade-out—another gesture of falling off, of descending—is added to the other forms of falling and descent that transform the piece. This, too, transforms both levels, infinite and finite. Toward the end of line 2, we can just barely make out in the acute region (registers 5–7) a nearly invisible and inaudible last apparition of the level agglomerate that was heard in that region at the beginning of the line. From this faint point to the end, the infinite level dissolves as well into the closing, speckled, drifting mist at the sonic center.

The transformation processes that were set in motion at the beginning of "Fall" have by the end wholly altered, indeed virtually pulverized and annihilated, its sonic texture.[4]

PHOTO 17
Robert Cogan: No Attack of Organic Metals
Performed by organist Martha Folts and assistants
Duration: 11 minutes 22 seconds

The novelist E. L. Doctorow, author of *Ragtime* and *Loon Lake*, has written that his own theories about his books are "no more qualified than anyone else's."[5] (I concur with this view in regard to my own work.) Similarly, with disarming honesty Mahler is reported to have said, "An artist shoots in the dark, not knowing whether he hits or what he hits."[6] These remarks reflect one side of the complex matter of artistic intention and realization—the side that acknowledges possibilities of uncertainty and doubt. What simple statement of intention is adequate for a compositional act covering months or years, and never (in any case) wholly conscious?

So the few comments that follow are not to be regarded as an authorized analysis. They are autobiographical comments—concerning not my life, but rather some of my thoughts in composing and reflecting on *No Attack of Organic Metals*.

In part, *No Attack of Organic Metals* (or *NAOM*) originated in the surprising idea that there exist many potential analogies between organ sounds and the sounds of our everyday electromechanical environment. Organ sounds themselves are to a certain extent electromechanical. A wind supply, originally powered mechanically or (nowadays) electrically, is controlled by a set of switching devices (including organ keys). When released by the proper switches, wind is powered through chosen pipes to produce the sounds we hear. Once switched on, an organ sound can continue unabated until it is switched off, or until the power fails. It is unaffected by human breath supply (as in singing and wind instruments), bowing fatigue (as in bowed instruments), or natural decay (as in plucked or struck instruments). Stravinsky complained: "The monster never breathes."[7] This can be a defect or a virtue. Stravinsky's remark, made while he was writing his *Symphony of Psalms,* assumed a context of other breath-dependent, decay-prone sounds. I, in contrast, assumed a context of other electromechanical sounds, as potentially unchanging and eternal as the organ's.

Unbreathing or superbreathing, organs in any case are ancient sound synthesizers. The various ranks of organ pipes each display different spectral and sonic characteristics. The ranks (also called *stops*) are grouped into *flutes, diapasons,* and *reeds.* An organ will have several slightly different variants from each category. The three groups correlate in general spectral character with the *sine, square,* and *sawtooth* wave sounds of recent electronic synthesizers.

Just as a synthesizer derives many different spectra and sounds from its basic wave forms, so does an organ from its groups of pipes. However, almost every instrument offers a different selection of stops. A reasonably complete organ will have two or three keyboards, plus a set of pedals, each having a sonic repertoire of a dozen different stops selected from the three basic groups. This gives a total repertoire of three or four dozen basic sounds, some similar, some dissimilar, which also can be combined to produce a great many more.

For a particular piece, an organist selects or creates one or more sounds from this sonic potential. The process of selecting stops (and thereby spectra and sounds) is called *registration.* Even when a composer offers registrational guidance, as is fully done in *NAOM,* the organist will still need to make many adjustments for each organ that affect the final sonic results.

In their capacity to produce a vast quantity of spectral formations and sounds, organs parallel and rival the electromechanical world. This is the second important analogy between organ sounds and those of the electromechanical environment, and an especially important one for *NAOM.*

A selection of electromechanical sounds appears on tape throughout the piece. In composing *NAOM,* I used them as sonic models, finding that these so-called noises offered a stimulating variety of sonic "sheens and grains."[8] I was attracted by all their sonic characteristics, from their spectral variety and complexity to their unchanging, eternal aspect; once unleashed, they seem able to go on forever.

While I was fascinated by the model sonorities, I did not then have the instruments to analyze their spectral formations. So the spectrum analytic process proceeded by ear and by thought. Gradually, with careful listening, the model sonorities began to give up some of their well-kept secrets—the ranges, quantities, spacings, and rubbings of their spectral elements. In the

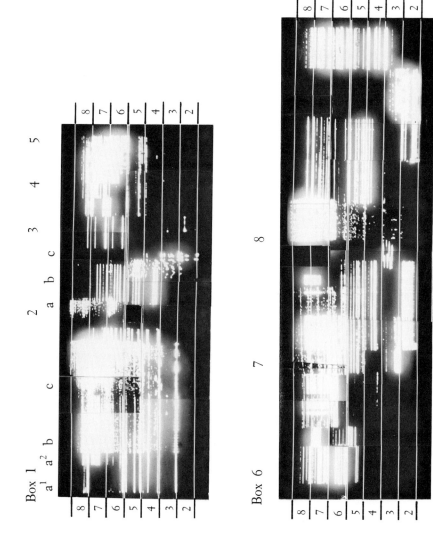

Photo 17. Robert Cogan, *No Attack of Organic Metals.*

Photo 17. Robert Cogan, *No Attack of Organic Metals.*

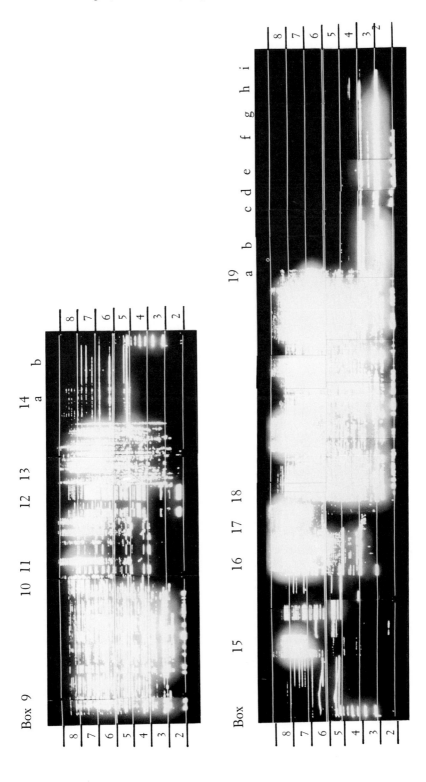

course of composition, the model electromechanical sonorities were brought into many kinds of interplay, both direct and long distance, with organ sounds related to them.

The interaction between the model sonorities and organ sounds can be observed in Photo 17. The beginning of the piece (see a^1–c in Box 1) show a simple instance of these interactions. In this passage the interplay proceeds in reverse order, so that the model sonority is gradually unveiled:

a^1, a^2 organ derivations from the model sonority;

    b a mixture of organ derivations and the tape model;

    c tape of the electromechanical model sonority alone.

The first organ sonority a^1, immediately seizes and presents the two most striking characteristics of the following model sonority, its internal opposition of low harmonic spectral strands, registers 3–6, to high, fully packed noise bands, registers 6–8 (compare a^1 and c). In the model sonority there is a dense, rapidly beating buzz of adjacent elements in register 8 (4,000–5,000 Hz); in a^1 this distinctive feature is separated and highlighted by a gap in registers 6–7 from the low, spaced harmonic remainder of the sonority.

Thus, the first sound of the piece isolates and focuses on these two internally contrasting elements of the coming model sonority. Only after these opposing spectral features have been isolated do the following sonorities (a^2 in the organ; b, a mixture of organ and the model sonority) fill in the spectral gaps. They lead finally at Ic to the complete presentation of the model sonority alone.

NAOM begins with the sonic essence, and then progresses to the inner details and totality of the electromechanical model. The spectral connections between the sonorities rivet the entire progression together. As they are presented in a single box of the notated score (Box 1), so too do they form a single spectral block in Photo 17.

To rivet the entire progression together; to shape a sonic world in which the organ and the electromechanical tape sounds contribute in equal and like measure—these were among my aims in composing *NAOM*. In Box 2 (Photo 17, line 1), the spectra are again knit together, but to attain a different goal. Tape and organ sounds alternate to form the single descending spectral contour that plunges from the highest to the lowest regions of the piece's spectral range (registers 9 to 1).

Later in *NAOM* we find, at a and b in Box 14, another passage in which a model sonority is juxtaposed with its organ derivations. In this case the model, an air-raid siren, precedes its organ derivations. The hint of an impurity, the major second C-D^5, in the otherwise harmonic spectrum of the siren (a in Box 14) is mirrored by major second impurities, D-E, implanted in the otherwise harmonic organ spectrum (b in Box 14). Once again, under analysis the spectra of both the electromechanical siren and the organ reveal several features in common (their D^5 fundamental; identical partials in regis-

Photo 17, Details b–i from Box 19.

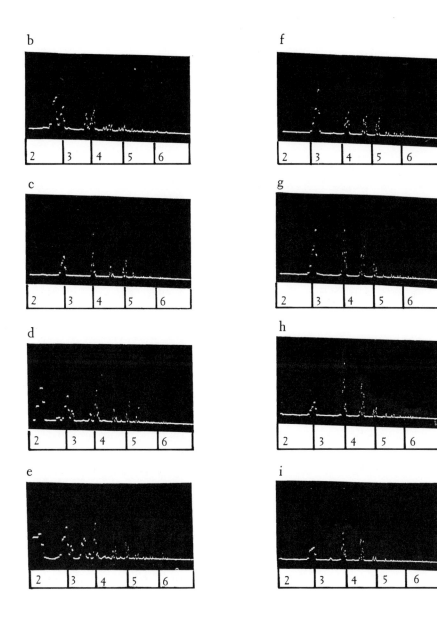

Fig. 33. Cogan, *No Attack of Organic Metals*, table of beats generated in Details *b–i* from Box 19.

```
b:              14 bps
              ┌─────────┐
             ┌110  124┐
      6 bps / │ A2  B2 │ \ 7 bps
            / └        ┘
          ┌─Ab2  Bb2─┐
          └104  117─┘                   Ab3 Bb3  B3
           └────────┘                   208 233 247
             13 bps                     └──┘ └──┘
                                       25 bps  14 bps

c:                              Bb3  B3              Bb4  B4
                                233 247             466 494
                                └───┘               └───┘
                                14 bps              28 bps

d:      Bb2 B2  C#3      C#3 Bb3  B3                 Bb4  B4
        117 124 139      208 233 247                466 494
        └──┘ └──┘        └──┘ └──┘                  └───┘
        7bps 15bps       25bps 14bps               28 bps

e: B1 C#2 Bb2 B2  C#3   F3  F#3       F4  F#4       Bb4  B4
   62 69  117 124 139   175 185       349 370       466 494
   └──┘ └──┘ └──┘        └───┘         └───┘         └───┘
   7bps  7 bps 15bps     10 bps        21 bps       28 bps

f:      Bb2 B2           Bb3  B3  F4  F#4           Bb4  B4
        117 124          233 247  349 370          466 494
        └───┘            └───┘   └───┘             └───┘
        7 bps            14 bps  21 bps            28 bps

g:  similar to f, but 14 bps very intense
h:  similar to g, but 7 and 28 bps weak
i:  similar to h, but fainter
```

ters 6–7; a comparable intensification of spectral elements in register 7) which rivet together another sonic succession.

The closing passage of *NAOM*, at Box 19, lets us draw a final sonic inference from the spectrum photo. This concerns sonic interference, which is heard as acoustic beats. Such beats are audible wherever spectral elements are adjacent—that is, where spectral elements virtually rub against each other. When this occurs, the spectral elements simultaneously activate the same portion of the inner ear, causing the interference known as *beats*.

Beats cannot be seen in spectrum photos; but wherever we see simultaneous adjacent spectral elements, or spectral bands, we can infer their existence. Details *b–i*, from the conclusion of *NAOM* (Box 19), show the presence in every sonority of pairs (at least) of adjacent elements that interfere with each other. The sonic result is the strong pulsating beats that dominate these sonorities.

Not only are beats dominant throughout the passage, but each minute change of spectral configuration alters the speeds and intensities of the beats. Each sonority produces a distinctive *nest* of beats, throbbing and pulsating at different speeds and intensities. Using the information provided in the details, the speeds of the various throbs and pulsations can be precisely calculated. Figure 33 translates the adjacencies in Details *b–i* into frequency numbers (Hz), and then calculates from them the numbers of beats per second (bps) evident in each complexly beating nest.[9]

From Figure 33 we observe that the beats pulsate at four principal different rates of speed; 7, 14, 21, and 28 bps. The fastest pulsations are multiples of the slowest ones. We find in the fourth of the eight nests, Detail *e*, the richest configuration of beats, as well as those with the greatest intensities. That nest and Detail *f*, the next one, include beats covering the entire gamut of beat speeds of this passage. Following these two climactic nests, the more extreme speeds of beats (the fastest and the slowest) grow progressively weaker. As the end of the piece approaches, the complexity of the nests and the general intensity of the beating are diminished. Beats, however, are never entirely extinguished in the conclusion of *NAOM*. Just as the piece began with rapidly buzzing beats in its very highest region (register 8), so it ends with slower throbs of beats in its very lowest region (registers 1–3).

Here, too, in this last example in the book, a spectrum photo reveals the existence of sonic relationships—identities, subtle connections, and oppositions—whose presence might hardly be suspected. The electromechanical sonorities that lie at the heart of *NAOM* cannot conveniently be notated in any other way. Nor is there another practical way of comparing the sonic models with their organ derivations. Now spectral analysis unlocks and displays, in Photo 17, a new world of potential musical sounds and of already realized sonic relationships. It is as effective in this new context as it has been in more familiar ones, revealing heretofore unnoticed sonic elements and levels of unexpected musical relationships. It makes available new degrees of sonic perception, and opens unexplored realms of musical experience.[10]

Part II
Tone Color: A Phonological Theory

La victoire avant tout sera
De bien voir au loin
De tout voir
De près
Et que tout ait un nom nouveau.

Victory above all will be
To see clearly afar
And all things
Up close
So that all, all bear a new name.

— GUILLAUME APOLLINAIRE

5.
The Theory of Oppositions

FOR ALMOST A century following Helmholtz's pathbreaking experiments, analysts of musical sound engaged in the exploration of single phenomena: the sound of a single instrument, or even of a single note of a single instrument. Not until the 1960s and 1970s were the first analyses of entire tone color contexts and entire musical works undertaken.[1] In these analyses, the vast amount of information that had been collected about single instruments was applied to instrumental groupings; but the process was cumbersome. The technology of spectrum analysis has changed that situation radically, making possible the analysis of entire contexts and works, and greatly increasing the speed and scope of such studies. Researchers need no longer depend on prior analysis of every individual instrument of a context; or guess about the spectral results when instruments are combined; or analyze musical works, sounds, or sonic properties piecemeal, except when this is advantageous. Part I gave an indication of the way in which the field of sonic research has expanded. Using the newly discovered techniques and information, it is now possible to begin to map and assess music's entire spectral tone color realm and to study the musics of a variety of cultures and epochs, with their panoply of diverse sonic media and approaches.

The following pages propose a framework for such analyses of tone color—a framework that is possibly more comprehensive than any that has yet been presented. There is a constant play of reflections between the analysis of individual musical works and the description of the full tone color realm; the latter is enriched by the former, and the resulting insights into tone color can be applied to other individual works. By this process of mutual reflection, our perspective both on individual works and on the entire tone color realm has been greatly enlarged.

The scope of the sonic realm, too, has turned out to be unexpectedly broad. Writing of depth in visual art (specifically in Cézanne), the French philosopher Merleau-Ponty once said: "We can no longer call [depth] a third dimension. In the first place, if it were a dimension it would be the *first* one . . . But a *first* dimension that contains all the others is no longer a dimension . . . Depth thus understood is, rather, the experience of everything in its place at the same time, a locality from which height, width, and depth are abstracted, of a voluminosity we express in a word when we say that a thing is *there.*"[2] No less is true of the spectral formations we have been observing. They *include* the melodic lines and registral fields of music's deployment in space, its harmonic textures, its rhythmic patterns and proliferations in time, as well as its instrumental and vocal sounds, and their combinations. In the end, to understand these spectral formations is to understand a large part of the totality of musical structure.

Consequently, a theory of tone color is necessarily (at least in part) a theory of musical structure. This is not to say that *only* spectra and their formations are relevant to musical structure; on the contrary, the world of music is large—larger than any one point of view. Musics can build their spectral formations using the pitches of various musical language systems (modal or tonal, asymmetrical or symmetrical, hierarchical or nonhierarchical) and using various rhythmic systems (metrical or not). Both of these domains, musical language and musical time, are rich and fascinating; but they are not complete in themselves. They also play a role in creating the spectral formations that ultimately include them. These spectral formations may provide an additional, or even the fundamental and necessary, motivation for their being. The sonic domain extends far beyond the music that previously was regarded as "coloristic." It may well include all music, and (at least potentially) all of music's parameters.

An important topic in Part I was sonic relationship. While we observed the spectral morphology of different sonic moments, we did not *merely* observe them. Within a given context we found that morphologies may resemble one another, may be transformations of one another, may oppose one another—or may do all those three at once. In these ways the different sonic morphologies interrelate; and out of these interrelationships emerges a spectral pattern, design, or shape that is an entire musical piece.

In the 1970s theorists observed similar relationships, which, unknown to them, resembled a form of relational analysis already developed in linguistics, specifically in phonology. This connection should cause little surprise. Linguistic phonology has aimed to define and understand the *sound shape* of language.[3] It aims to clarify the *relationships* of sounds in a language, and of sound in language.[4] It strives to define the sound shape of each extant language, and the place of each in the broad system of language sounds. In a comparable way, Part II will proceed from the sound shape of individual musical works to the place of each work and shape within the broad system of musical sounds. Both domains, language and music, seek an understanding of the structural role of sound.

In Part I we saw that the structure of numerous pieces depends upon sonic *oppositions*—that pieces flow between oppositions which define their beginnings, endings, and principal points of arrival and demarcation. In linguistic theory, too, oppositions play an essential role. In their book *The Sound Shape of Language*, Roman Jakobson and Linda Waugh begin by quoting the American philosopher C. S. Peirce: "A thing without oppositions *ipso facto* does not exist."[5] Jakobson's colleague, N. S. Trubetzkoy, had already launched his *Principles of Phonology* with an elaboration of the same idea:

> The concept of distinctiveness presupposes the concept of *opposition*. One thing can be distinguished only from another thing: it can be distinguished only insofar as it is contrasted with or opposed to something else, that is, insofar as a relationship of contrast or opposition exists between the two. A phonic property can therefore only be distinctive in function insofar as it is opposed to another phonic property, that is, insofar as it is a member of an opposition of sound.[6]

The philosophical roots of this idea extend back far beyond Peirce—indeed, to the very beginnings of European philosophy. To Anaximander, founder of Greek philosophy and author of the first known maps of the earth and cosmos, has traditionally been attributed the view that "the differentiation of opposites is the origin of existing things."[7] Heraclitus, shortly afterward, conceived of unity itself as a play of opposites: "There would be no harmony without high and low nor any living creatures without the opposites male and female."[8] From Anaximander, Heraclitus, and Plato to Hegel (whose entire philosophy was dialectical) and Peirce, the significance of oppositions remains one of the constant motives of philosophy. Oppositions—for example, the grave/acute opposition to which we have already devoted much attention—form the structural basis of all of phonology.[9]

The proposals that follow build upon the oppositional observations of the individual sonic analyses in Part I (and their predecessors), and upon the rich experience of linguistic phonology in assessing sonic oppositions. A *table of oppositions*, modeled on those used in phonology, is proposed as a way of interpreting spectral phenomena and of encompassing music's entire tone color domain. Such a table is constructed so as to include all spectral distributions and the full panorama of available tone color characteristics. A composer makes choices among the opposing features—choices that chisel away certain of the total (and contradictory) possibilities of the sonic medium. The significance of these choices can be seen by comparing sonorities and contexts. In the end, the specific morphology of each sonority and the sound shape of each context stand revealed.

The table may, of course, turn out to be incomplete; other oppositions than the thirteen it proposes could be deemed useful in the future. Still, its thirteen oppositions allow for inclusion of virtually every form of fundamental sonic contrast that we have so far observed. Whether or not these thirteen oppositions prove in the future to be definitive, their presentation here cannot but help composers and theorists achieve a fuller awareness of sonic possibilities. Some of the specific oppositions in the table resemble those of linguistic phonology. Even those with similar names, however, have been defined here to fit their musical, rather than their linguistic, functions.

THREE SAMPLE TABLES

The four remarkable synthesized sonorities that introduce Babbitt's *Ensembles* (Photo 15) are characterized in the four columns of our first sample table of oppositions (see Figure 34). Each sonority is evaluated there in terms of the thirteen available sonic oppositions.

Any sonic moment represents not a single sonic property, but rather a *bundle* of choices from a whole set of sonic possibilities. Comparably, in linguistics the smallest independent linguistic moment—the phoneme—has been designated by Jakobson and Waugh as "a set, bundle, totality . . . of concurrent sound properties."[10] Figure 34 includes the thirteen opposing characteristics by which every musical sound distinguishes itself in its sonic context: characteristics of spectral placement and scope, density, dynamics, envelope, tone modulation, and interference phenomena.

In each of Babbitt's sonorities (or in those of any other musical context) each of the thirteen oppositions can be represented by its negative (−) or positive (+) pole; by a mixture of them (∓); or by an intermediate, neutral state (∅). The decision as to whether a characteristic is negative or positive has not been arbitrary. The negative forms are *low* energy states: low spectral frequency, low intensity, low activity, low internal contrast. The positive forms are *high* energy states: high spectral frequency, high intensity, high activity, high internal contrast. For example, registrally *grave* (lower frequency) is negative, whereas *acute* (higher frequency) is positive. *Narrow* spectrum (low internal contrast) is negative; *wide* (high internal contrast) is positive. In density, *sparse* is negative; *rich* positive.

For its thirteen distinct sonic features, the table records the orientation, negative or positive, of each sonority. In this way, *negative* and *positive* themselves assume the role of meta-features. At the base of each column are totals of the negative and positive features of each sonority.

The comparison of sonorities and sonic contexts can take several forms, depending on whether one looks at individual oppositions or broader sonic levels. As we saw in Chapter 4, the four sonorities form a directed spectral flow as they progress from mixed-register spectral distributions to an increasing focus on the registral extremities, first high and then low. This progression is summarized in the grave/acute line of the table: ∓, ∓, +, −.

On the larger scale, it is apparent that the four sonorities move steadily from dominance of the positive pole to dominance of the negative. This progression can be observed in two interrelated ways. First is the growth of purely negative features: −3, −5, −5, −9. Second is the changing relative balance between negative and positive features in the totals, as shown in the graph in Figure 34; from +2 (*a*), to −2 (*b*), to 0 (*c*), to −6 (*d*). Almost every sonic characteristic progresses to its negative pole in the final sonority. Simultaneously, the positive characteristics diminish toward zero. The sonic transformation to grave registers in sonority *d* is consequently amplified by the numerous parallel transformations to negative forms in almost every sonic

Fig. 34. Table of oppositions for Babbitt, *Ensembles for Synthesizer,* Introduction.

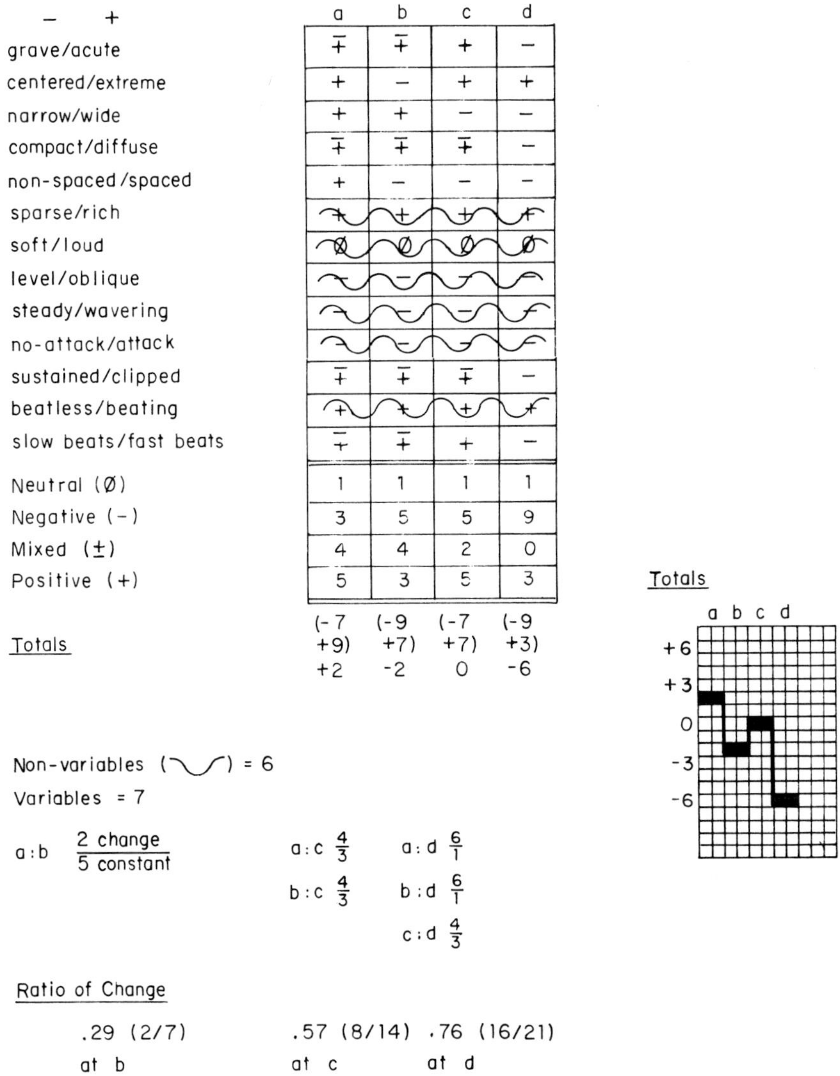

− +	a	b	c	d
grave/acute	±	±	+	−
centered/extreme	+	−	+	+
narrow/wide	+	+	−	−
compact/diffuse	±	±	±	−
non-spaced/spaced	+	−	−	−
sparse/rich	~	~±	~+	~
soft/loud	~Ø	~Ø	~Ø	~Ø
level/oblique	~	~−	~	~
steady/wavering	~	~	~−	~
no-attack/attack	~	~	~	~
sustained/clipped	±	+	±	−
beatless/beating	~+	~±	~+	~
slow beats/fast beats	±	+	+	−
Neutral (Ø)	1	1	1	1
Negative (−)	3	5	5	9
Mixed (±)	4	4	2	0
Positive (+)	5	3	5	3

Totals

	a	b	c	d
	(−7	(−9	(−7	(−9
	+9)	+7)	+7)	+3)
	+2	−2	0	−6

Totals

Non-variables (~) = 6

Variables = 7

$a:b$ $\dfrac{2 \text{ change}}{5 \text{ constant}}$ $a:c\ \dfrac{4}{3}$ $a:d\ \dfrac{6}{1}$

$b:c\ \dfrac{4}{3}$ $b:d\ \dfrac{6}{1}$

$c:d\ \dfrac{4}{3}$

Ratio of Change

.29 (2/7) .57 (8/14) .76 (16/21)

at b at c at d

feature. The structural evolution of the progression can be most inclusively described not simply by its registral transformations, as telling as those are, but by the entire coordinated set of transformations to negative sonic characteristics in its closing sonority.

We see in this instance how analysis of the sonic features in terms of negative and positive oppositions reveals how an entire context is shaped. The Babbitt introduction displays a two-step progression from positive (+2) to negative (−6) over intermediate sonorities (−2 and 0). This transformation is especially vivid in the graph in Figure 34.

Fig. 35. Table of oppositions for Berg, *Wozzeck*, Act III, Scene 2, measures 109–116.

− +	a	b	c
grave/acute	−	∓	∓
centered/extreme	−	+	+
narrow/wide	−	+	+
compact/diffuse	−	−	+
non-spaced/spaced	〜	〜	〜
sparse/rich	−	+	+
soft/loud	−	+	+
level/oblique	−	−	+
steady/wavering	−	−	+
no-attack/attack	−	−	+
sustained/clipped	−	−	+
beatless/beating	−	+	+
slow-beats/fast beats	Ø	−	+
Neutral (Ø)	1	0	0
Negative (−)	12	7	1
Mixed (∓)	0	1	1
Positive (+)	0	5	11
Totals	(−12, +0) −12	(−8, +6) −2	(−2, +12) +10

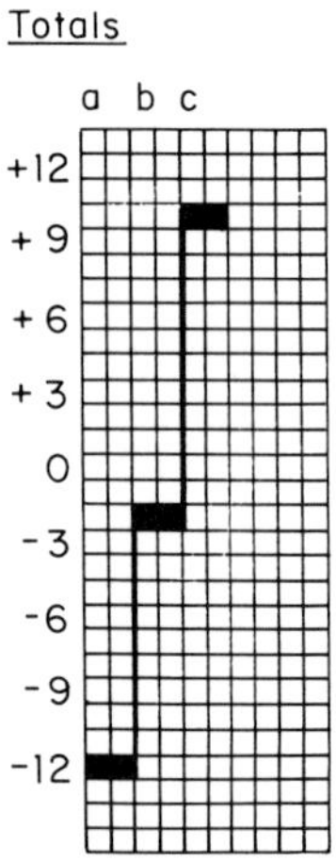

Totals

A contrasting example can be seen in Figure 35: a table of oppositions for the climax of Berg's *Wozzeck* (Photo 13). Its first phrase (the first half of the photo) progresses from an overwhelmingly negative to an overwhelmingly positive sonic character—from −12 to +10 (where 13 is the ultimate limit in either direction). In this phrase, heretofore often regarded as the very prototype of the static, the sonic moments at the beginning and end reveal a precise and strikingly complete sonic reversal. The midpoint, −2, is almost exactly the mean value between the sonic extremities.

Far from being static, the phrase emerges as a clearly shaped, directed, and coordinated set of transformations. In contrast to Babbitt's sound shape, from positive to negative, Berg's progresses from negative to positive. The transformational processes work equally freely in both directions, which is a potential source of great richness and variety.

Very different musics can reveal similar underlying formative processes. Figure 36 shows the famous Introduction to Stravinsky's *Le Sacre du Printemps*.[11] Its beginning at −11 is very similar to the intensely negative beginning of Berg's climactic passage. The table shows that the entire Introduction effects a gradual sonic transformation whose goal is the massive orchestral pulsations that begin the "Danses des Adolescentes" (columns *e–f*), with their clear, positive sonic reversal at f. In *Le Sacre*, as in the pieces by Babbitt and Berg, between the opposing extremities we find intermediaries which effect a sonic transition. In *Le Sacre* this transformation function is borne by several entire phrases (columns *b–e*), reflecting a slower, more elaborated process.

The table of oppositions offers a model of how whole sets of sonic characteristics combine and work together to create sensations of *direction* of sonic transformation, either increasingly negative or increasingly positive. Many insights accrue from the analysis and comparison of these passages. To begin, one realizes how striking intensely negative sonic character is. (Intensely positive sonic character is, of course, a powerful force as well—but that seems less astonishing.) It provides a fitting goal for Babbitt's transformations, and it creates an ear-catching beginning for both the Berg and Stravinsky examples, two of the most famous passages of all twentieth-century music. Perhaps Saint-Saëns phrased his comment about the beginning of *Le Sacre* incorrectly: he should not have said "What *instrument* is that?" but "What a rare *sonic character* is that!"

Passages like these from Berg and Stravinsky cover an immense sonic ground. Berg's phrase traverses 22 sonic degrees (from −12 to +10), while Stravinsky's traverses 17 (−11 to +6). These spans are to be measured against an optimal maximum of 26 degrees (−13 to +13)—a figure that, however, may represent only a theoretical absolute, rather than a realistically attainable goal. Babbitt, by comparison, effects a powerful sonic change by a swift transformation of only 8 degrees (+2 to −6).

In evaluating a sonic context, the *process of change* itself—for example, its *speed* and *distance*—can be as revealing as the direction of change, negative or positive. This process is revealed in part by the *ratio of change*, indicated at the bottom of Figure 34.

The ratio of change is calculated by comparing the exact morphology of each sonic moment, in terms of each feature, with the morphology of every previous sonic moment. We must realize that the process of change has several aspects. There is, for example, *local* change: constancy (or contrast) between each feature in *adjacent* sonorities. And there is *global* change: constancy (or contrast) between each feature in *all* the previous sonorities, adjacent and distant. Global change not only involves the comparison of dis-

Fig. 36. Table of oppositions for Stravinsky, *Le Sacre du Printemps*, Introduction and "Danses des Adolescentes," beginning.

− +	a	b	c	d	e	f
grave/acute	∅	−	−	∓	∓	∓
centered/extreme	−	−	−	−	+	+
narrow/wide	−	−	+	+	+	+
compact/diffuse	−	−	−	−	∓	+
non-spaced/spaced	−	+	+	+	−	−
sparse/rich	−	−	−	+	+	+
soft/loud	−	−	−	−	+	+
level/oblique	⌇	⌇	⌇	⌇	⌇	⌇
steady/wavering	⌇	⌇	⌇	⌇	⌇	⌇
no-attack/attack	−	−	−	−	−	+
sustained/clipped	−	−	−	∓	+	+
beatless/beating	−	−	+	+	+	+
slow beats/fast beats	∅	∅	−	−	+	+
Neutral (∅)	2	1	0	0	0	0
Negative (−)	11	12	10	7	4	3
Mixed (∓)	0	0	0	2	2	1
Positive (+)	0	1	3	4	7	9
Totals	(−11, +0) −11	(−11, +1) −10	(−10, +3) −7	(−9, +6) −3	(−6, +9) +3	(−4, +10) +6

Totals

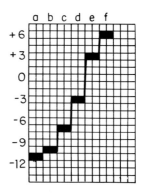

tant points, but also shows the results of the entire accumulating process of change.

The calculations in Figure 34 first compare every feature of every sonority with every feature of every previous sonority for constancy or change. In terms of local relationships, the adjacent sonorities of Babbitt's progression show gradual increasing change:

	a:b	b:c	c:d
change	2	4	4
constant	5	3	3

(These measurements take only the seven *variable* features of the context into account; the six nonvariables in Babbitt's context play no part in these calculations. This is consistent with the linguistic principal of contextual determination of features: the nonvariables are never factors of change.) At the same time, the calculations reveal that the transformations carry the sonic character ever further away from the quality of the first sonority. This is seen by comparing sonority *a* with each succeeding sonority:

	a:b	a:c	a:d
change	2	4	6
constant	5	3	1

The ratio of change is a calculation of the total quantity (and total quality) of change represented by any sonic moment, compared to all that has preceded it. It is figured by comparing all the features of all the previous sonorities with which any point can be compared, near and far. This global change might, consequently, be regarded as an index of overall sonic "freshness" in a given context. (The ratio can range between 0, no change, and 1, total change.)

In the Babbitt Introduction, the ratios of change indicate how special the last sonority is in comparison to the sonorities that precede it. The last sonority displays by far the highest ratio of change, .76, compared with .29 and .57 for the preceding sonorities. Not only is the last sonority the most distant from the first sonority in sonic characteristics (six features changed, only one constant); it is also reached by an accelerating momentum of sonic change, represented by the soaring ratio. Maintaining an increasing ratio of change in an evolving context, and thereby increasing sonic freshness, is neither a common nor a trivial compositional accomplishment. This increasing ratio sums up, by taking every sonic feature and transformation of the phrase into account, all of the changes of sonic quality (direction and distance together) in the Introduction to Babbitt's *Ensembles*.

The table of oppositions makes possible, then, wholly new insights into the formation of Babbitt's context. These include the realization that it is shaped by a single overriding direction of sonic transformation, positive to negative; and that it is transformed by measurable amounts of sonic change, local and global, as the passage unfolds. Local change increases from one sonority to the next, and global change intensifies as the progression moves from its beginning to its end. Sonic processes previously unrecognizable and undefinable emerge as precisely, imaginatively shaped.

6.
Specific Oppositions

PRIOR TO DEFINING the specific sonic features that appear in the table of oppositions, one general point must be clarified. In their definition and in their use, the oppositions are to be regarded contextually and relatively, rather than absolutely. Only by reference to its own specific context can a sound be judged grave or acute, narrow or wide, soft or loud. What is grave in one context might be acute in another. Compare, for example, the music of the Balinese shadow-play (Photo 5) with the Tibetan Tantric chant (Photo 2). In the shadow-play *gamelan*, the spectral elements in register 4 (supplied by the *gendèr* fundamentals) are grave, forming the bass of the spectral structure. On the other hand, in the context of the ultra-low bass voices of the Tibetan chant, the spectral elements in register 4 are among the acute features of the men's voices. Consequently, spectral elements in register 4 bear opposing functions in the two contexts—grave in one, acute in the other.

This usage agrees with an aspect of linguistic practice that was clarified by Trubetzkoy: "It is a basic fact of phonology that the phonemic content of a phoneme depends on the position of the phoneme in the phonemic system and consequently on the structure of that system. Since the systems of distinctive oppositions differ from language to language and from dialect to dialect, the phonemic content of the phonemes also varies according to the languages and dialect."[1] The role of an element depends on its context.

Contextuality bears, as well, on the question of analytic precision. In referring to spectral analyses as *photos,* we speak metaphorically as well as literally. By varying the adjustments of the sound spectrum analyzer, we can produce a variety of analytic readouts. The adjustments represent a variety of *focuses,* which produce analytic pictures of varied detail, emphasis, and breadth. As Wittgenstein observed, no absolute analytic precision exists.[2] However, in our contextual, relative practice, analytic variance (to be problematic) would have to be so great that it would upset an entire context. It would have to alter an entire system of relationships—for example, by rendering a grave sound as acute.

Once again Jakobson and Waugh have foreseen the problem: "From time to time the tabulation of distinctive features meets with imaginary arguments which question the accuracy of measurements and the degree of descriptive precision. These objections are in most cases based on the substitution of a crude metrical attitude for a sane, relational, topological treatment."[3] The analyses presented here are likewise relational and topological, as in the spectrum photos.

Let us now consider in detail the thirteen contrasting sonic features of the table of oppositions.

1. *Grave/acute.* The spectrum of every sound will activate some part of the sonic space of its context. As the proportion of spectral energy in the grave region increases, the sonic character becomes relatively duller and darker. As the proportion of spectral energy in the acute region grows, the sonic character becomes relatively brighter. In linguistic structures this contrast is primary—for example, grave versus acute vowels. As we have seen, such contrasts are extraordinarily important in music as well.

The potential audible range covers approximately ten registers. However, the judgments here are based on the actual range that is spectrally activated in the full context of a musical work. This is often a much more limited space. The total spectral range of a specific musical work is divided into three equal parts: grave, neutral, and acute (see Figure 37).

The designation *grave* (−) indicates activation of some part of the grave space. The designation *acute* (+) indicates activation of some part of the acute space. The designation *grave-acute* (∓) indicates activation of both the grave and acute spaces simultaneously. The designation *neutral* (∅) indicates activation of neutral space only.

2. *Centered/extreme.* The extremities are the outer halves of the grave and acute regions of a spectral context (see Figure 38). The designation *centered* (−) indicates activation of neither extremity. The designation *extreme* (+) indicates activation of any part of either extremity (or of both extrem-

Fig. 37. Division of any spectral range into grave, neutral, and acute regions.

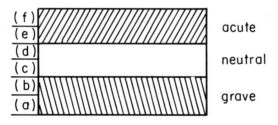

Fig. 38. Division of any spectral range into centered and extreme regions.

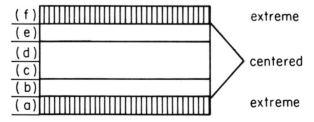

ities). The opposition *extreme/centered* is a measure of degree of spectral shading. *Extreme* designates the most intense (intensely dark, or intensely bright, or their mixture) spectral shades of a specific sonic context. *Centered* designates the less intense spectral shades.

3. *Narrow/wide*. This opposition refers to the distance between the outer spectral elements of a sonority or sonic context. The designation *narrow* (−) indicates a distance between a sonority's outer spectral elements of half the width (or less) of the total spectral context. The designation *wide* (+) indicates a distance between a sonority's outer spectral elements of more than half the width of the total spectral context.

Where a total spectral context spans six registers, a narrow sonority will span three registers or less, measured from its outer elements. A wide sonority will span more than three registers. The opposition narrow/wide is one measure of spectral, sonic complexity, since a wide sonority contains more different (or more widely differentiated) registral characteristics than a narrow one. The opposition narrow/wide is not identical to centered/extreme. Whereas wide sonic moments are often also extreme, a narrow moment can be either centered or extreme, depending entirely on its registral placement. Consequently, we are dealing with two independent variables: centeredness and width.

4. *Compact/diffuse*. Whereas the opposition narrow/wide refers to the total width of a sonority or sonic context, compact/diffuse refers to the width of each individual spectral element. Each spectral element can be either a compact partial strand, or a more diffuse, widely spread band of "noise."

The designation *compact* (−) indicates a spectrum formed of strands of partials, each reading out as a single frequency or pitch. The designation *diffuse* (+) indicates a spectrum formed of bands covering more than one frequency or pitch ("noise" bands). The mixed designation *diffuse-compact* (∓) indicates a spectrum formed simultaneously of both strands and bands. *Diffuse* spectra, since they include adjacent frequencies, necessarily produce acoustic beats (see definitions 12 and 13, below).

5. *Non-spaced/spaced*. This distinction refers to the possible presence of a spatial gap between spectral elements within a single sonority or sonic context. Generally, the designation *non-spaced* (−) indicates the presence of no gap wider than one octave between adjacent spectral elements (strands or bands) of a sonority. The designation *spaced* (+) indicates the presence of a gap wider than one octave.

Certain sonorities of a clarinet, often described as "hollow-sounding" because of the absence of even-numbered partials, are evidence of the spaced feature (see Figure 39). The judgment non-spaced/spaced is especially dependent upon context. A spaced spectrum is any that contains significant gaps compared to the other spectral formations in the context.

6. *Sparse/rich*. This is a density distinction: a sparse moment or context is spectrally less dense than a rich one. To establish spectral density, we compare the quantity of simultaneous elements of any sonority or sonic context with the maximum number of simultaneous elements to appear anywhere in

Fig. 39. Messiaen, *Quatour pour la Fin du Temps*, "Abîme des Oiseaux," measure 41. This detail (whose fundamental is B^{b3}) with its total omission of the second partial and suppression of the third and fourth partials, displays the spaced feature of certain clarinet sonorities.

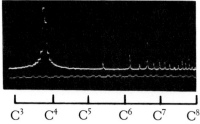

the context. (The distinction is defined somewhat differently for a sonority consisting of compact elements than for a sonority consisting of diffuse elements.)

In a *compact* sonority (formed of spectral strands), the designation *sparse* (−) indicates the presence of half (or less than half) the maximum number of partials found in any sonority of the context. The designation *rich* (+) indicates the presence of more than half the maximum number of partials found in any sonority of the context.

In a *diffuse* sonority (formed of spectral bands), the designation *sparse* (−) indicates the presence of bands whose width is half (or less than half) that of the maximum band width found in any sonority of the context. The designation *rich* (+) indicates the presence of one or more bands whose width is more than half that of the maximum band width found in any sonority of the context.

For *compact-diffuse* (mixed) sonorities (∓), the judgment sparse/rich follows the general lines indicated above.

Thus, in a context where eighteen simultaneous partials is the maximally rich sonority (see Photo 13), a sonority of nine partials or less is sparse. However, in another context (see Photo 2), a sonority of nine partials is rich.

Just as the distinction narrow/wide is a measure of one aspect of spectral, sonic complexity (the number of different, or widely differentiated, registers brought into play at one sonic moment), so the distinction sparse/rich is a measure of another aspect of spectral, sonic complexity (the number of different individual sonic elements superimposed in one sonic moment). Furthermore, like the diffuse feature, the rich feature generally implies the presence of acoustic beats. The beats are produced by adjacencies, which are created when musical space is richly filled by spectral strands or bands.

The single sine tone is the ultimate of sparseness; "white noise" is the ultimate of richness. Earlier tone color analyses, which drew attention to the opposition of sine-tone-like to white-noise-like spectral configurations, can now be understood as examples of the sparse/rich opposition.[4]

In the commentary to Photo 14, it was shown that there exist two pairs of density distinctions: compact/diffuse refers to the density of the spectral element, while sparse/rich refers to the density of the full sonic moment or context. Compact, sparse indicates minimal total density; diffuse, rich indicates maximal total density.

7. *Soft/loud.* Like musical space, the dynamic range of music can be divided into thirds: soft, neutral, loud. Musical notation gives a very rough approximation: *ppp–p*, *mp–mf*, and *f–fff*, respectively. The sone count offers a more exact measure for doubtful cases.[5] For example: 1–10 (soft), 11–40 (neutral), 41–130 (loud). These measures are approximate, and are for illustration's sake only. An appropriate scale can be constructed for every context.

The designation *soft* (−) indicates a sonic moment or context whose total loudness is *pp–p* (or softer). The designation *loud* (+) indicates a sonic moment or context whose total loudness is *f–ff* (or louder). The designation *neutral* (∅) indicates a sonic moment or context whose total loudness is between *p* and *f*.

Where loudness fluctuates greatly within any single sonic moment or context, such a case can be indicated (∓). The same indication can be used for a context that systematically includes such dynamic contrasts within each sonic moment.

8. *Level/oblique.* This distinction deals with the general pitch orientation—whether fixed or moving (sliding) in musical space—of each spectral element. The designation *level* (−) indicates a spectral element whose frequency (pitch) remains generally fixed throughout its duration. The designation *oblique* (+) indicates a spectral element whose frequency (pitch) is generally changing (either ascending or descending or both) in the course of its duration—*glissando*, for example. A mixed designation, *level/oblique* (∓), indicates the simultaneous presence of both level and oblique spectral elements in a sonic moment or context.

It is not always easy to assess the fixity or motion of diffuse banded (noise) spectra. When doubt arises, they can be considered *level-oblique* (∓), reflecting both the uncertainty and their complex, quasi-random state.

9. *Steady/wavering.* This distinction refers to frequency microfluctuation (its absence or presence) in the course of a spectral element. For example in pitch vibrato, the general pitch orientation can remain level while microfluctuations occur at the rate of 5–20 per second.

The designation *steady* (−) indicates a spectral element without observable microfluctuations of frequency (pitch). Note that such a spectral element can be level, or oblique—moving without microfluctuation in either direction. The designation *wavering* (+) indicates a spectral element displaying microfluctuations of frequency (pitch). The mixed designation *steady-wavering* (∓) indicates the simultaneous presence of both steady and wavering elements in a sonic moment or context. The same ambiguity that renders diffuse elements *level-oblique* (∓) also renders them *steady-wavering* (∓).

10. *No-attack/attack.* This distinction refers to the onset of the spectral elements of a sonic moment or context. The distinction depends on whether or not there is a noticeable difference between the onset and the continuing body of the spectral elements. It is possible for an onset to be so distinctive

and separate that it can be regarded as an autonomous sonic moment. The distinction we are dealing with here, however, refers to sonic moments where noticeable attack does, or does not, combine with other continuing sonic features.

The designation *no-attack* (−) indicates the absence of any noticeable difference between the onset of the spectral elements of a sonic moment and the continuing body. Observe that we are dealing with *noticeable* differences. Considered in isolation from a context, almost every onset might display some differences from the sonic body that follows. However, in musical contexts (due to overlapping, masking, and other factors) many onset details disappear for all practical purposes (see the spectrum photos).

The designation *attack* (+) indicates the presence of noticeable differences between the onset of the spectral elements of a sonic moment and the continuing body. Sometimes the noticeable difference will comprise additional partials; sometimes it will include diffuse bands (in linguistic consonants or pizzicato attacks, for example); and sometimes it will comprise greater (or lesser) intensity of some or all of the spectral elements. These suggestions do not exhaust the possibilities (see Figure 40).

11. *Sustained/clipped.* This distinction deals with the relationship of the body to the release of the spectral elements. Here it is a question of the timing of the release, and especially of the presence (or absence) of a gap of silence within a spectral context—for example, between a spectral element and its continuation.

The designation *sustained* (−) indicates that spectral elements contain

Fig. 40. Japanese shakuhachi repertoire, *Depicting the Cranes in Their Nest*, details. Contrasting spectra of the onset (above) and body (below) of a single note (G⁵) from this piece. The onset reveals a strongly audible, brief G⁴, as well as a host of other spectral distinctions.

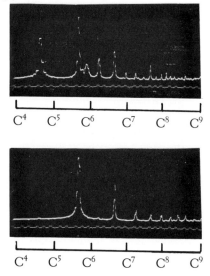

no interior gaps of silence, and follow one another without noticeable gaps of silence. The designation *clipped* (+) indicates that spectral elements display interior gaps of silence, or display gaps of silence as they succeed one another. The mixed designation *sustained-clipped* ($\mp$) indicates that some spectral elements reveal gaps of silence while others do not.

What is regarded as the repeated attack of a sonority is often more accurately seen as interruption of the sonority by gaps of silence—in other words, as *clipping*. This is especially so when the repeated onsets do not reveal noticeable attack elements. Such a situation would be regarded as no-attack, clipped. The essence of the clipped feature is silence—the substitution of silence for one or more previous spectral elements.

12. *Beatless/beating.* This distinction deals with the absence or presence of acoustic beats in a sonic moment. Acoustic beats are not visible in the spectrum photos. Since they are generally produced by pitch adjacencies, they result wherever close adjacencies appear in a spectrum. Consequently, they are common in diffuse sonorities, and in rich ones as well; but they are by no means limited to these. The slow beats known as *choral effect* appear wherever voices or instruments double a musical gesture, producing spectral doublings with slight discrepancies of pitch. These are, in effect, very narrow adjacencies. But they are too close for the spectrum analyzer or its display (and often for the ear as well) to resolve separately.

The designation *beatless* (−) indicates the absence of close spectral adjacencies and of spectral doublings, so that no beats appear during a sonic moment or context.

The designation *beating* (+) indicates the presence of close spectral adjacencies and/or of spectral doublings, so that beats exist during a sonic moment or context.

13. *Slow beats/fast beats.* This is the sole opposition that is wholly dependent on another opposition: it comes into play only when distinction 12 is beating (+). The speed of beats depends upon the frequency difference between close adjacencies. A^4 at 440 and 441 Hz, simultaneously, produces 1 beat per second (bps).[6] One bps is the slowest speed of beating. At the other extreme, beats of more than 200 bps can be noticed. Slow beats produce a sonic wavering or undulation (wa-wa-wa). Rapid beats add a tingling or buzzing feature to a sound or context.

The designation *slow beats* (−) indicates the presence of beats of a speed generally between 1 and 50 bps. Such beats can be produced especially by choral effect, or by adjacencies in registers 0–4. The designation *fast beats* (+) indicates the presence of beats of a speed generally between 50 and 250 bps. Such beats can be produced especially by adjacencies in registers 5–10. The mixed designation *slow beats–fast beats* ($\mp$) indicates the presence of both slow and fast beats. When a passage is beatless (distinction 12) distinction 13 is given as *neutral* ($\emptyset$).

The above distinction between slow and fast beats is not entirely contextually defined, but it will apply in most situations. It can be redefined contextually (and simplified) as follows: *slow beats* are those produced by choral effect and by adjacencies in the lower half of a context's spectral range; *fast beats* are those produced by adjacencies in the upper half of a context's spectral range. Since diffuse bands are completely filled by adjacent frequencies that produce beats, one or more diffuse bands in the lower half of a context produce slow beats and in the upper half produce fast beats. Diffuse bands in both halves produce a mixture of slow beats and fast beats.

7.
Parenthetical Issues

A NUMBER OF questions are raised by the process of defining sonic oppositions. These questions are as much general and philosophical in nature as they are specific and operational. They may not, however, be of interest to everyone; readers who wish to follow only the main lines of the presentation should feel free to proceed to Chapter 8.

The Time Span of a Sonic Moment. When a sonic moment is characterized in terms of the thirteen oppositions, does that moment cover a single, fixed, knowable duration? For purposes of this book, it does not. Any characterization lasts as long as the context maintains that character. Every sonic character requires *some* span of time to establish itself. That span is different in different contexts.

One analyst of musical sound, Wayne Slawson, has suggested that the concept *tone color* be limited so as to eliminate changes that occur over time.[1] He would have us regard all such changes as rhythmic, or as successions of two or more different tone colors and spectral moments. He would equate a tone color only with a single spectrum.

Such a solution to the problem is tempting, but has already been shown to be untenable. Every sonic phenomenon requires some duration; but each may require a *different* minimum duration for its existence. This is undeniably true of spectral elements, generated as they are by sound waves of different frequencies—in other words, of different durations. Where a low-frequency pitch like E^1 (about 40 Hz) is present in a spectrum, each of its waves requires 1/40 of a second. However, a mid-frequency wave of 400 Hz $(G–G^{\#4})$ requires only 1/400 of a second, and a high-frequency wave of 4,000 Hz (B^7) only 1/4,000 of a second. In practice, for any of these frequencies to be audible, a minimum of approximately five waves is required. Still, in the time required for the low-frequency pitch, ten of the mid-frequency pitches and one hundred of the high-frequency pitches can occur. Consequently, while one low-frequency pitch is coming into being, many high-frequency features can change. High-frequency spectral elements, attack features, and beats can all come and go, or undergo transformation. Even while one spectral element is establishing its existence, others will appear and disappear, or undergo simultaneous mutation.

Therefore, in musical contexts there can exist no single, unchanging, meaningful instant of time that can be unambiguously isolated and analyzed. Scientists have already recognized this situation with respect to visual phenomena, and indeed to all physical phenomena. As E. H. Gombrich wrote: "The *punctum temporis* (a razor-like unextended instant in time) could not even show as a meaningless dot, for light has a frequency." And Karl Popper has noted that, "owing to optics, there cannot be in physics a state of the world at an instant of time."[2]

Analyzing sonic phenomena means analyzing spans of time that display diverse sonic features. The features have a variety of orientations—in musical space, in intensity, in time. Although the spectral features are paramount, they generate other derived features such as acoustic beats. The concept of oppositions offers an inclusive means of showing the constructive, interactive role of each and all of them in time—the time of the musical work.

In practice, the absence of an unchanging sonic moment (or any other absolute reference) means that analysts can choose the time span that undergoes analysis. This is true, for example, with respect to the variable settings of the spectrum analyzer and its photographic display, which can present a sonic context in greater or lesser detail. It is also true in interpreting the spectrum photos, where the analyst can choose those spans whose features are then characterized in terms of oppositions. The criterion for such choice is not absolute but relative: how *revealing* any choice is about a particular context. The analyses presented here strive to illuminate all of the different, or at least principal, tone colorings by observing those changing sonic moments (shorter or longer spans) that are characteristic of a context. There is no absolute or prior certainty that the choices made are the right ones. Nor is there any absolute standard according to which they are the wrong ones. Insight, especially growth of insight, is all.

Oppositions and Instruments. Musicians have become accustomed to think of tone color in terms of musical instruments—the tone color of a violin, or of a shakuhachi. Yet far from having one overall sound, each of these instruments is a storehouse of an unusually rich variety of sounds. The ultimate example of such sonic diversity is the root instrument of all human sound, the human voice. It is the source not only of a virtual infinitude of languages of varying sound shapes, but also of equally rich and varied traditions of sung sound.

The habit of equating tone color with seemingly fixed and immutable instrumental colors was reinforced in recent European music history by the late-nineteenth- early-twentieth-century myth of instrumental perfectibility. The instruments and instrumental sonorities of that period were regarded as the perfect realizations of earlier strivings. This view was so prevalent that the earlier "imperfect" instruments and their sonorities were often consigned to oblivion.

Only in recent decades have musicians in the European tradition realized how intimately the structure of a given music and the sounds of its original instruments are connected. Indeed, the spectrum studies in Part I are a new tool for demonstrating this profound connection (see especially Photo 6) and for confirming the realization that instrumental sounds are diverse rather than fixed. Instruments, even the "same" instrument in different historical periods and different contexts, are sources of diverse features and play varying roles in the structural sonic oppositions.

In this respect, instruments are analogous to linguistic phonemes and the letters that represent them. As Jakobson and Waugh have observed: "The question 'what is the opposite of the English [m]?' makes no sense. There is no unique opposite. But the feature *nasality* finds its true and single opposite in the *absence of nasality*."[3] Likewise, the question "What is the opposite of the violin?" makes no sense. One must observe its specific contributions to a particular spectral and sonic context, and formulate the structure of that context. One might then observe the opposition of its wavering vibrato to other steady elements; or of its diffuse pizzicato attack to other compact, no-attack elements (to mention only two of the violin's sonic properties that might contribute distinctive features). To approach the same subject from the opposite direction, the features wavering, diffuse, and attack are not the exclusive provenance of the violin. Many different instruments display these features in different contexts, and the violin itself sometimes displays them and sometimes does not.

Necessarily, then, our focus is on the sonic context and its structure, which the instrument helps create. This emphasis on the acoustic result (as opposed to the articulatory, instrumental means) finds its anticipation, too, in linguistics. "It is not the movements of the speech organs but the speech sounds themselves which are primary in language," wrote Alexander Thomson.[4] Jakobson and Waugh emphasize this point: "Discrete articulated sounds did not exist before language, and it is pointless and perverse to consider such 'phonic stuff' without reference to its linguistic utilization. The growth of language and the development of the human supra-laryngeal vocal apparatus are interconnected innovations."[5]

Researchers will find this attitude invaluable when thinking about the relationships between instruments and tone color. It will cause them to re-evaluate those conclusions of psychophysical testing which rest on the assumption that instrumental recognition and tone-color perception are identical.[6] Moreover, it will encourage them to revise a long tradition of conceiving music's sonic aspect, its tone color, only in terms of combinations and successions of instruments, as in "orchestration." It is not the musical instruments but the musical sounds themselves which are primary in musical structure and expression.

Essential Sonic Relations and Functions. Here we must come to grips with an elusive, subtle problem. Fortunately, it is one that has been at the center of linguistic discussion for several decades, so we can profit from the experience of that field.

If we consider a single sonic moment—for example, a given sonority in a musical work—each realization of it (different models of the same instrument, different players, different physical environments, and so forth) will produce slightly but noticeably different spectral details. In Photo 6 we saw an extreme example of such differences between the fortepiano and the modern grand piano. On a smaller scale, the problem recurs everywhere: no two sonic moments are ever exactly alike. Yet amid the differences, we can usually recognize the first measure of, say, Beethoven's Piano Sonata Opus 109. So, too, we usually recognize a word or phrase (in a language we know), whether it is pronounced by a man or woman, adult or child, spoken, sung, or whispered, despite all of the attendant physical differences.

Given the physical, spectral diversity of different instruments, performers, performance traditions, sonic environments, and so forth, how do we maintain the identity of a piece? The answer may prove surprising to many readers. In linguistics it has become clearer through a distinction made by Trubetzkoy (among others) between two different approaches that he named the *phonetic* and the *phonological*. Phonetics, in his view, is "the study of sound pertaining to the act of speech—the science concerned with the material aspect of sounds of human speech. The speech sounds that must be studied in phonetics possess a large number of acoustic and articulatory properties. All of these are important for the phonetician." Phonology, on the other hand, is "the study of sound pertaining to the system of language. The system of language as a social institution constitutes a world of relations, functions, and values. The linguistic values of sounds to be examined by phonology are abstract in nature; they are above all *relations, oppositions,* etc. The phonologist needs to consider only that aspect of sound which fulfills a specific function in the system of language."[7]

It might seem that these definitions accord primacy to phonetics, for its task is to recognize and encompass every physical aspect of every speech sound; however, this means that it must deal with much that is inessential and even accidental—for example, sounds that tell us the sex and age (perhaps also the nationality and regional dialect) of the speaker, the speaker's idiosyncrasies of speech, and even accidental speech features of the moment. Since phonetics deals with speech sounds alone and not with linguistic relations and functions, it cannot even tell which of the sounds it discovers have specific functions, for those can only be determined by an examination of phonic functions—the province of phonology.

Whereas phonetics has revealed the inchoate sonic stuff residing in speech, phonology has discerned the specific functions of particular sounds in linguistic utterances and languages. It has also discerned the way in which speech sounds interrelate to form the sound shape of specific languages and of human language in general. It has done this by concentrating on those phonic features that distinguish one meaning from another in a language (the *distinctive features*) and by observing and postulating the pairings of those features into specific recurrent oppositions.

Phonology has developed a theoretical model, the system of linguistic oppositions, which organizes the sonic stuff of phonetics in terms of functions, relations, and values. This model shows that we recognize a word or phrase by attending not to every phonetic detail of sound, but rather to certain constant oppositional functions and relationships that distinguish one meaning from another.[8]

There is much here for the analyst of musical sound to ponder. Since Helmholtz, traditional musical phonetics has developed through the study of single instruments, attempting to specify all the articulatory and acoustic aspects of single instrumental sounds. Like phonetics, it has unearthed much revealing information.

The success of such study, especially in recent years as it has become technically refined, has inevitably led to further questions. For example, what is the musical value of the newly discovered sonic properties? How do they interrelate in specific musical situations? It has sometimes been assumed that by continuing the same processes of investigation, the answers to these questions will emerge. Another dimension has been added to the questions by the use of the same information in electronic music to create quasi-instrumental sounds—an ideal "trumpet" or "piano," for example.

It has not been widely observed that these latter questions enter a new domain (that is, they take a new logical form). In linguistics it is the domain of phonology—of values (what is the musical value of a given sonic property of an instrument?), relationships (how do given sonic properties interrelate?), and function (what is the function of a given instrumental sonic property?). The ideal trumpet, too, represents a value judgment, and often a functional one as well.

The experience of linguistics suggests that the essential sonic features of any musical instrument are not finally to be discovered either in the practice room or in the anechoic chamber, or even in the most sophisticated statistical or technical analyses of instrumental sound isolated in those places. Rather, the essential sonic features of any musical instrument are to be found in the sum total of its structural sonic contributions to musical contexts. These features will be revealed by analyzing the functions and relations of those contexts and of the instruments in creating them.

This realization does not diminish the value of phonetic-like analyses of musical instrumental sounds. It does, however, require adding several significant levels to their interpretation. As a specific example, consider the sonic onset. Many instruments reveal, in noncontextual, phonetic-like analysis, a fleeting onset sonority (attack noise, for example) that is different from the continuing body of sound. In the Japanese shakuhachi, some stressed attacks include an instant of sound an octave lower than the continuing body of the sound (see Figure 40). Where this quality is audibly and noticeably present, as it often is in solo shakuhachi music, it can add such features as grave, extreme, wide, rich, attack, and clipped to the sonic contexts. In the large repertoire of solo shakuhachi music, where this attack element can be clearly perceived, attacks make a significant contribution to the sonic structure. By contrast, the European flute attack sometimes includes an instant of sounds in lower and higher octaves than those of the continuing body of its sonority.[9]

This attack does not always seem to make a significant sonic contribution to its contexts. Indeed, it very often disappears in the instrumental ensemble context of much European music, where it is masked by the sounds of other instruments. To be musically and sonically significant, a sonic element must reveal itself in a musical context. Indeed, it requires not only presence but, usually, reiteration and amplification (used here in the structural sense). Some phonic properties are so weakly (or accidentally) present in an instrumental sound and so unamplified in a given context that they disappear in the context or do not, at any rate, characterize it. They do not *function* in the particular context.

Much of what happens in the musical sonic context represents chosen values. A composer (or performer) selects certain sonic qualities to be emphasized or suppressed at a given moment. Although these qualities must be available in the sonic repertoire of the instruments employed, their appearance or nonappearance is determined by structural sonic choices made by the creator. In doing so, creators sometimes discover new instrumental sonic capabilities. The sound of an instrument may not be *infinitely* malleable, but it is *significantly* malleable—individually, contextually, and historically. In a variety of contexts it will convey a variety of sonic functions, relations, and values. The sonic essence of the instrument will be established by observing in musical contexts the entire range of its malleability and constancy.

The analyst of a musical context likewise makes choices by picking the sonic contexts to be analyzed and the oppositions to be considered. The analyst must also define the total sense of the sonic unfolding and transformation of a given musical context: its sonic structure. At every stage, then—composition, performance, and analysis—choices are made and phonological work is carried out. The choices are the human, musical, phonological ones of selecting sonic functions, relations, and values. It is through such choices that the sonic essence of a music is attained and revealed.

Thus, in analyzing the sound shapes of various musical contexts and works, this book has necessarily moved beyond the processes of phonetics to those of phonology. It has also moved beyond the mere physical representation of the analyses (which is in fact never *merely* physical, for it already embodies numerous human choices) to an explicitly human level of analysis and understanding. It joins, and conjoins, science and art as essentially human ways of conceiving a world.

If linguistics is any guide, musical contexts and the system of musical sounds—like the system of language sounds—can be analyzed in no other way.

8.
Archetypes

THE TABLE OF oppositions is a way of conceiving and interrelating the smallest details of musical sound within the largest possible structural framework—that is, within the entire context of a musical work and all of the sonic possibilities available to it. Such minutiae as the spectral elements, flashes of attack noise, the pitch waverings of vibrato, and pulsations of acoustic beats are all included within it. In fact, almost all of its features depend on accretions of such infinitesimal elements, as they mass themselves into powerful structural and expressive forces. At the same time, the tabulation of oppositions reflects not only the existence and significance of such details, but also their mapping against the full available ranges of human hearing and perception—or, at least, against as much of those ranges as are included in any given work. For example, specific spectral elements are mapped within the complete audible range of the work; any specific speed of acoustic beats is mapped against the full range of beats, from slow to fast, appearing in the work; and so forth. This is all part of an effort to map, using the musical equivalents of the microscope and the telescope, the full range of phenomena of the sonic cosmos, whether of an individual work or of all music. It is an attempt, as in Apollinaire's verse, "To see clearly afar / And all things / Up close . . ." An inevitable aspect of such a vision, at once broadened and concentrated, is giving new names to the phenomena so recognized and located: "So that all, all bear a new name."

Spectrum photos, as revealing as they are, are not ends in themselves; they are invaluable sources of information for further structural judgments and insights, of the kinds attempted here in the commentaries and the tables of oppositions. Insight is all. The process of drawing insights from the sonic icons fashioned by humans in almost every culture and era is endless, and endlessly fascinating.

In conclusion, let us look once again at the sweep of the entire process. Spectrum analysis makes known a level and quantity of sonic detail (the spectral elements) previously hardly recognized in the analysis of musical contexts. From the immense array of sonic detail that the photos provide, we can draw conclusions about the significant features. Those features stand revealed in the opposing choices that characterize any moment of a sonic context. Furthermore, by comparing the complete sonic profile of characteristic moments of a musical work, we can observe the design of the entire context in terms of the largest oppositions: the poles of negative and positive sonic character, and those of constancy and change.

Having done this, certain archetypes of sound shape emerge. They are not the only possible archetypal designs, or even necessarily the best; they represent certain recurrent possibilities of design of the sonic medium. Observing them may stimulate the imagination of composers and theorists to discover still others.

Negative and Positive Sonic Characters

Foremost among these archetypal designs are the unidirectional transformations from negative to positive and from positive to negative. A negative to positive transformation underlies Berlioz's "Tibi omnes angeli" (Photo 11), just as it did the climax of Berg's *Wozzeck* (Photo 13) and the Introduction to Stravinsky's *Le Sacre du Printemps*. A positive to negative transformation, on the other hand, underlies Mozart's "Confutatis" (Photo 10), as well as the Introduction to Babbitt's *Ensembles for Synthesizer* (Photo 15). (Tables of opposition for the works discussed here can be found in Appendix B.)

A number of examples enact and then reverse the transformation, so that it moves from negative to positive and back again. These include Ligeti's *Lux Aeterna* (Photo 4), Debussy's "Nuages" (Photo 12), and Risset's "Fall" (Photo 16). Such a design can also begin positive, moving to negative and back again; this is the design of each line of Varèse's *Hyperprism* (Photo 14).

"Qui sedes, Domine" (Photo 1) displays an interesting variant of this last design. It retains its initial positive character and refers to it intermittently, even as a transformation to the negative is unfolding. This might best be regarded as comprising two simultaneous strata; one constant positive and one moving from positive to negative. Such a polyphonic design is especially interesting, given the monophonic texture of Gregorian chant. It shows a way of achieving structural density even in the face of textural simplicity. And such a design suggests further possibilities for a polyphony of archetypes—or for an archetype of polyphony.

Transformations characterized as unidirectional (from negative to positive, or the reverse) need not be monolithically so. The line of sonic transformation can be as elaborate—as full of comings and goings, curves and hesitations, momentary interruptions and returns, foreshadowings and echoings, as any other line. At its core, however, will be found an underlying, far-reaching, orderly increase or decrease of the negative or positive characteristics.

Here, too, we must recognize the overriding significance of context. The organ polyphony in flute-stops whose features constitute the beginning negative pole of Berlioz's "Tibi omnes angeli" would not be the negative pole in Ligeti's *Lux Aeterna*. Nor would the sustained choral texture whose features constitute the climactic positive pole of *Lux Aeterna* constitute the climactic

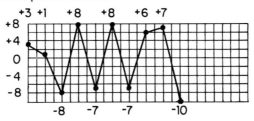

Fig. 41. Stravinsky, *Three Pieces for String Quartet*, Piece II, graph of the oscillating totals of opposing negative and positive features.

positive pole in the multichoral-orchestral ensemble of "Tibi omnes angeli."

Furthermore, the number of negative or positive features that constitutes the polar extremity can be different in different contexts. In "Nuages," 0 is the positive extremity, whereas at the climax of *Wozzeck* it is +10. Even where the number of negative (or positive) features that defines a pole is the same in two different contexts, the composer's selection of specific negative (or positive) features can be very different. All of this testifies to the extraordinary richness and malleability of the sonic domain. Even a single archetype finds innumerable different embodiments.

Compared to these archetypal designs, Stravinsky's *Piece II* for string quartet (Photo 17) displays an interesting and different design archetype. Beginning at a relatively neutral point, it oscillates between negative and positive extremes (see Figure 41). Instead of a gradual transformation from one sonic character to the other, there is an intense fluctuation between the opposing characters. This might be regarded as another instance of the archetypal polyphony present in "Qui sedes, Domine."

Such a design is the sonic equivalent of the alternation between two different strata of rhythmic pulsation—the pulses MM (metronome) = 152 and MM = 228—that has been found to underlie the same movement.[1] Indeed, the oscillations of rhythmic pulsation and sonic character move in tandem, reinforcing each other. As might be expected, the faster pulsations (MM = 228) and the positive sonic strata (+3 and higher) coincide, while the slower pulsations (MM = 152) and the negative sonic strata (+1 and lower) are paired. In this way, the rhythmic and sonic formations of the movement, as well as their structural coordination, reveal the multilevel stratification that Edward Cone has pointed out as being especially and specifically Stravinskian.[2]

The polyphony of archetypes, or the archetypes of polyphony, takes on a different embodiment in the *Pemoengkah* (Photo 5). The sonic profile of this piece, once established, is relatively unchanging. It would be a serious mistake to regard this as evidence of a simple or (worse) primitive sonic formation. In this context, space gaps in register 4, and especially in register 6, define three separate, simultaneous sonic contexts, each displaying a distinct morphology. The sonic contrasts are not revealed over time, but are unfolded and partitioned throughout space. Of the three simultaneous sonic strata, the lowest two establish the negative pole (−6, −4); the highest establishes the positive pole (+4). What makes this especially noteworthy is that the highest stratum, forming the positive sonic pole, is *purely* spectral. It receives no reinforcement from fundamentals, which are entirely lacking in its registers (7 and 8). The existence of this stratum and its opposition to the negative lower strata might seem, therefore, to be elusive if not highly speculative. But in fact, it is just this stratum that bears the tingling, jangling sonic features that indelibly establish the unique sonic character of the *gamelan*. A stratified, polyphonic reading of this kind is necessary and revealing when the separations of sonic character are consistently spatial, not temporal.

CONSTANCY AND CHANGE

It is easier to describe archetypal designs of the opposing sonic characters negative and positive than those of the opposing sonic processes of constancy and change. Still, some general observations on the latter are pertinent.

The constancy or change of any sonic moment must be viewed in at least two perspectives: local and global. Local means comparison with the immediately preceding sonic context; global means comparison with all of the preceding sonic contexts of a piece. The introduction to Babbitt's *Ensembles* showed that a succession of small changes in the local perspective can add up to significant sonic change in the global perspective.

The greatest constancy occurs when both perspectives show little change. In that case, there is change in relatively few sonic features in adjacent morphologies, and a low ratio of change in the global perspective. The greatest change occurs when it is present to a large extent in both perspectives. In that case, there is change in relatively many sonic features in adjacent morphologies, and a high ratio of change in the global perspective.

The two perspectives, local and global, are quite independent of each other, which can be illustrated by comparing two moments of Debussy's "Nuages," Stages 4 and 6 in the photo (see Table 2). In the local perspective, Stages 4 and 6 both display very little change from their preceding stages: Stage 4 changes only two features, Stage 6 changes none. (There are orchestration changes between Stages 5 and 6 that justify considering Stage 6 a new stage, even though no features change.) Stage 6, despite its complete lack of local change, still displays slightly greater change than Stage 4 in the global perspective. This is due to the introduction, in Stage 5, of significant sonic change, which persists in Stage 6. The ratio of change of Stage 5, .54, is

Table 2. Comparison of two moments in Debussy's "Nuages."

	STAGE 4	STAGE 6
Features	2 changing	0 changing
	11 constant	13 constant
Ratio of change	.39 (14/36)	.43 (26/60)

among the highest of the entire movement. The appearance of pizzicato strings is unforgettable for anyone who has heard "Nuages." The changes of Stage 5 maintained in Stage 6 continue to lend it sonic freshness.

The independence of the local and global perspectives can be confirmed in another way. A massive local change is not always imposing in the global perspective. This is especially true when there is a sudden *return* to a previously dominant set of sonic features. The suddenness of the return makes for great local change; but the returning quality itself will usually reduce the amount of global change.

Sonic change is a subtle matter. It is always necessary to keep the two perspectives, local and global, in mind.

Of course, it is possible for two sonic morphologies to display the same *total* negative or positive orientation, yet show a different distribution of the specifically negative and positive features. In this case there is change but no movement, in either the positive or negative direction. This occurs in Berlioz's "Tibi omnes angeli" between c and d in Photo 11. Both sonic moments have a similar neutral orientation $(-1, 0)$ in this context. They function as transitional midpoints within the example's sweeping transformation from a strongly negative sonic character (-12) to a positive one $(+6)$, a transformation covering 18 sonic degrees. Despite their similar orientation and function, there is considerable *local* change between c and d: five changing features, eight constant. The changing features make a significant contribution to the ratio of change, which is .49 at d.

The highest ratio of change in the Berlioz segment, .57, is found at the arrival at the positive pole $(+6)$, at f. Interestingly, this moment shows relatively little local change from its preceding moment, e: only two changing features, eleven constant. How is it that such a vivid sense of global change is accomplished there?

To produce vivid global change with relatively little local change, the two new features at f must carry a very high charge of change in terms of all the preceding contexts; they must be very rare in those preceding contexts. In the Berlioz, that is the case. The two new characterisics, the diffuse and oblique features of the cymbals and bass drum, are introduced only at this climactic positive moment and have not previously appeared in the piece.

Just as two different sonic morphologies can add up to the same, or a very similar, total negative or positive orientation, so can two different instrumentations produce very similar sonic morphologies. Several passages of "Nuages" illustrate this. We have already noted the similar features and total morphologies of Stages 3 and 4. Stage 4 doubles woodwinds and French horns with the stringed instruments of Stage 3. The only resulting change of features is the dynamic transformation from neutral to loud. Stage 4 is, consequently, merely an intensification of features already present in Stage 3. Similarly, the transfer of the melody from bassoons to muted cellos (a-b in Stage 8) does not significantly alter features throughout Stage 8, which remain virtually constant.

So we see that slight orchestrational or instrumental changes can sometimes cause great sonic change, as in "Tibi omnes angeli," or can cause virtually no sonic change even on the local scale, as in "Nuages."

It is always of special interest, and sometimes very surprising, to learn which feature (or features) bears a high charge of change in a particular sonic context and musical work. At the close of Risset's "Fall" (Photo 16), a set of features new to the movement appears. Consequently, they bear a very high charge of global change and give its conclusion an unusually high ratio of change, .70 (see d in Photo 16). The four late-appearing sonic features are neutral register (grave-acute $\emptyset$), centered, diffuse, and non-spaced. These oppose earlier characteristic features of the piece: grave and acute registers (+ and −), extreme, compact, and spaced. The new features are so highly charged with change that the high ratio of change is attained even though the movement is at that moment returning to its initial negative character (−4). This shows, strikingly, how the close of the piece looks both backward and forward.

It is the sonic structure of this piece's particular contexts that makes the appearance of these features so telling. Concentration in the neutral registral region is not, a priori, sonically vivid. On the contrary, in much other music it is sonically ordinary. The same is true of the non-spaced feature: much music proceeds without space gaps; but in this piece, where spacing is common, non-spaced is the unusual feature, bearing a strong charge of change. The context defines the significance of the features. Sometimes it does so in ways that are very unexpected, and it is context that creates the unexpected.

A similar example can be found in Stravinsky's *Piece II* for string quartet (Photo 7). In the course of its oscillation between sonic extremes, certain features remain rare: grave or neutral register alone (absence of acute), centered, and narrow. The appearance of two or more of these features together produces a moment of intense sonic change in the piece: at d^1, h, and j in Photo 7. Almost always, these moments consist of a single note softly sustained in a low register. The piece closes with such a sonic morphology, a recurrence of moment d^1. As in Risset's "Fall," the power of Stravinsky's conclusion is embodied in the freshness and strong charge of change of the final sonority. It is a contextual power, rather than an innate one. It is important for both the composer and theorist, not to mention the perceptive listener, to understand which sonic features bear that potential charge of change in each piece's specific context.

Conclusion

WITH THE AIM of increasing understanding by composers and theorists, performers and listeners, this book has traced and followed the sonic creative and analytic processes. To analyze is to create a map or model—a model that reveals certain functions and relationships. Since the functions and relationships here have been sonic ones, the model is a phonological one. A model itself can be verbal, numerical, or graphic, and the preceding chapters have employed (to varying degrees) all of these means: commentaries, tables of oppositions, and spectrum photos. When creating and using an analytic model, it is wise to remember Gregory Bateson's admonitions: "The map is not the territory" but a way of "organizing news of differences in the 'territory.' "[1] Through maps we find our way to the rich experiences of the world, to the sonic as to any other. Using the map as a starting point, we can further refine and develop the experiences to which it leads and can improve the quality and relevance of both the mapping and the experience.

Throughout music's history, the relationship between music and sound has been more than a little curious. Music is the art of sound, and sound stands at the heart of music's power and order. Yet music's sonic flesh and substance have been oddly unnameable. Not until quite late in its history has it become possible to approach, picture, and name its sonic essence.

Having begun the process, we can understand some of the difficulties. The map must ultimately range in scope from extremely minute and fleeting sonic details to complete shaped contexts lasting minutes or hours. It must coordinate fine features of the physical world with subtle responses of the biological and mental worlds. Its range of historical periods and global cultures is correspondingly great. The magnitudes of difference are huge. The possibilities of losing one's way are considerable.

Still, it is possible to return from this terra incognita with initial pictures and names, which will undoubtedly be refined and enriched by later explorers. Sonic qualities previously unrecognized emerge in visible, identifiable order, illuminating musics that have been at once moving, fascinating, and mystifying. That the unknown realm of musical sound is vast and fertile has now become abundantly clear. Within its newly envisioned boundaries, and among its newly glimpsed details and forms, myriad discoveries lie ahead.

Appendix A
Spectral Analysis and Spectral Display

THE PRODUCTION OF the sonic images found in the spectrum photos followed the path shown in Figure A.1. This path led from a sound source through the spectrum analyzer to the display tubes, and then to the cameras which preserved the spectral images appearing upon them.

The source of musical sound could be either a recording or live voices or instruments. The spectrum analyzer was a thirty-three-millisecond fast Fourier transform instrument, capable of analyzing sounds in five contiguous octave registers simultaneously. The analyst could tune into the specific registers activated by the sonic media. For a given analysis, any five adjacent registers in the human audible range could be chosen. Neighboring registers were always examined as well. This was done to ensure that every analysis included the full range of significant, observable spectral elements. Different settings of the dynamic controls were also tested in order to bring out as much as possible of the existing spectral detail.

In the analytic sequence, the samples generated by the spectrum analyzer appeared simultaneously on two different display tubes. In one display appeared an ever-changing succession of details, approximately fifteen of them per second, in which spectral elements were represented as vertical spikes whose heights corresponded to their relative intensities. A stop control allowed for holding, studying, and eventually photographing any single spectral moment.

The second display was the source of the spectrum photos. This tube did not show a set of disconnected single spectral moments, but retained in a single frame the changing spectra of an entire passage. The analyst, through the scan controls, could change the time (and thereby the amount of analytic detail) contained in a single frame. On this display, time unfolded horizontally, while musical space—the five octave registers chosen for analysis—extended vertically. Each spectral element appeared as a strand or band, depending on whether it comprised a single frequency, or several adjacent frequencies banded together; and each spectral element appeared as a horizontal or a diagonal, depending on whether it was fixed in pitch or sliding. In the spectrum photos made from this display, the boundaries of the five octave registers are delineated by white horizontal lines that extend all the way across the photos. A double horizontal line indicates 1,000 Hz, at the boundary between registers 5 and 6.

Fig. A.1. Diagram of the spectral analysis and display procedure.

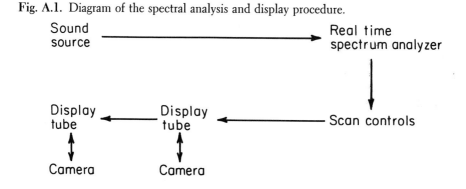

A number of the spectrum photos (6a, 14, 15, and 17) break the five-octave registral barrier of the spectrum analyzer. This was accomplished by producing two complete analyses covering different registers of the same work, and then combining them. In this way, up to ten registers (virtually the entire audible range of humans) could be scrutinized. To do this required different settings of the register and dynamic controls of the two analyses As a result, the intensities of the two analyses that were combined were not absolutely compatible, and the analyses might embody slight distortions. No claim can be made for absolute accuracy, which in any case does not (and cannot) exist. The chosen procedures made it possible to reveal and examine the spectral detail of particularly wide-ranging musical works.

One can only look forward with great anticipation to future developments of this technology. Ideally, every complete-context spectrum analysis should cover the entire audible space range, respond to the full audible dynamic range, and precisely display the relative loudnesses of all the spectral elements more or less as they are received and perceived by the human auditory system. The technological advances have been large, but several steps are still needed before that ideal can be attained. Moreover, these analyses are not merely technical. Progress in this field depends upon the continuing coordination of technology with conceptual science and artistic understanding.

Appendix B
Tables of Opposities

Fig. A.2. Gregorian chant, "Qui sedes, Domine" (Photo 1).

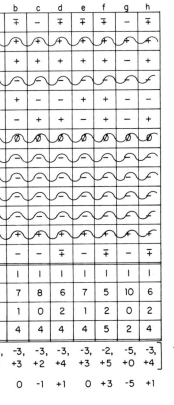

− +	a	b	c	d	e	f	g	h
grave/acute	∓	∓	−	∓	∓	∓	−	∓
centered/extreme								
narrow/wide	+	+	+	+	+	+	−	+
compact/diffuse								
non-spaced/spaced	−	+	−	−	+	+	−	−
sparse/rich	+	−	+	+	−	+	−	+
soft/loud								
level/oblique								
steady/wavering								
no-attack/attack								
sustained/clipped								
beatless/beating								
slow beats/fast beats	∓	−	−	∓	−	∓	−	∓
Neutral (Ø)	I	I	I	I	I	I	I	I
Negative (−)	6	7	8	6	7	5	10	6
Mixed (∓)	2	1	0	2	1	2	0	2
Positive (+)	4	4	4	4	4	5	2	4
Totals	−3,	−3,	−3,	−3,	−3,	−2,	−5,	−3,
	+4	+3	+2	+4	+3	+5	+0	+4
	+1	0	−1	+1	0	+3	−5	+1

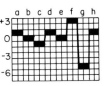

157 TABLES OF OPPOSITIONS

Fig. A.3. Gyorgy Ligeti, *Lux Aeterna* (Photo 4).

− +	a	b	c	d	e	f	g	h	i	j	k	l	m
grave/acute	Ø	Ø	+	−	∓	∓	−	∓	−	−	∓	−	−
centered/extreme	−	−	−	−	−	+	−	+	+	−	−	+	+
narrow/wide	−	−	−	−	+	+	−	+	+	−	+	+	−
compact/diffuse	−	−	−	−	−	−	∓	−	−	−	−	−	−
non-spaced/spaced	−	−	+	−	+	−	+	+	−	−	+	+	−
sparse/rich	−	−	−	−	−	+	−	+	+	−	−	+	−
soft/loud	−	−	Ø	−	Ø	Ø	Ø	+	−	−	+	−	−
level/oblique	−	−	−	−	−	−	−	∓	−	−	−	−	−
steady/wavering	−	+	+	−	+	+	+	+	+	+	+	+	+
no-attack/attack	～	～	～	～	～	～	～	～	～	～	～	～	～
sustained/clipped	～	～	～	～	～	～	～	～	～	～	～	～	～
beatless/beating	−	+	+	+	+	+	+	+	+	+	+	+	+
slow beats/fast beats	Ø	−	−	−	−	∓	−	∓	−	−	−	−	−
Neutral (Ø)	2	1	1	0	1	1	1	0	0	0	0	0	0
Negative (−)	11	10	8	12	7	5	9	2	8	11	7	7	10
Mixed (∓)	0	0	0	0	1	2	0	4	0	0	1	0	0
Positive (+)	0	2	4	1	4	5	3	7	5	2	5	6	3

Totals

$$\begin{bmatrix} -11, & -10, & -8, & -12, & -8, & -7, & -9, & -6, & -8, & -11, & -8, & -7, & -10, \\ +0 & +2 & +4 & +1 & +5 & +7 & +3 & +11 & +5 & +2 & +6 & +6 & +3 \end{bmatrix}$$

	a	b	c	d	e	f	g	h	i	j	k	l	m
	−11	−8	−4	−11	−3	0	−6	+5	−3	−9	−2	−1	−7

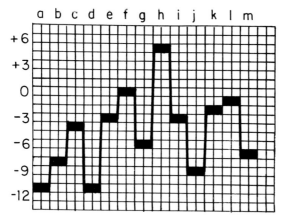

Fig. A.4. Balinese shadow-play music, *Pemoengkah* (Photo 5).

− +	a	b	c
grave/acute	−	Ø	+
centered/extreme	+	−	+
narrow/wide	+	−	+
compact/diffuse	∿	∿	∿
non-spaced/spaced	−	−	+
sparse/rich	−	−	+
soft/loud	Ø	Ø	Ø
level/oblique	∿	∿	∿
steady/wavering	∿	∿	∿
no-attack/attack	−	+	−
sustained/clipped	−	+	+
beatless/beating	+	+	+
slow beats/fast beats	−	∓	+
Neutral (Ø)	1	2	1
Negative (−)	9	7	4
Mixed (∓)	0	1	0
Positive (+)	3	3	8

Totals

$$\begin{bmatrix} -9, & -8, & -4, \\ +3 & +4 & +8 \end{bmatrix}$$

$$-6 \quad -4 \quad +4$$

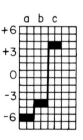

Fig. A.5. Stravinsky, *Three Pieces for String Quartet,* Piece II (Photo 7).

− +	a	b	c	d	d'	e	e'	f	g	h	i	j	k
grave/acute	∓	+	∓	∓	∅	∓	+	+	∓	∓	∓	−	∓
centered/extreme	+	+	−	+	−	+	+	+	+	−	+	+	+
narrow/wide	+	+	+	+	−	+	−	+	+	−	+	−	+
compact/diffuse	−	∓	−	+	−	+	−	∓	∓	−	∓	−	∓
non-spaced/spaced	−	+	−	−	+	+	−	−	−	−	−	−	+
sparse/rich	+	−	−	+	−	+	−	+	+	−	+	−	−
soft/loud	∓	−	−	+	−	+	∓	+	+	−	+	∓	−
level/oblique	∓	−	−	+	−	∅	∓	−	∓	−	−	−	−
steady/wavering	−	−	∓	−	+	∅	−	−	∓	∓	+	+	+
no-attack/attack	∓	+	−	+	−	+	−	+	+	−	+	∓	∓
sustained/clipped	+	+	−	+	−	+	−	+	+	−	+	−	+
beatless/beating	+	−	−	+	−	∅	−	+	+	−	+	−	−
slow beats/fast beats	+	∅	∅	+	∅	∅	∅	+	+	∅	+	∅	∅
Neutral (∅)	0	1	1	0	2	4	1	0	0	1	0	1	1
Negative (−)	3	5	9	2	9	0	8	3	1	10	2	8	4
Mixed (∓)	4	1	2	1	0	1	2	1	4	2	2	2	3
Positive (+)	6	6	1	10	2	8	2	9	8	0	9	2	5
Totals	−7, +10	−6, +7	−11, +3	−3, +11	−9, +2	−1, +9	−10, +4	−4, +10	−5, +12	−12, +2	−4, +11	−10, +4	−7, +8
	+3	+1	−8	+8	−7	+8	−6	+6	+7	−10	+7	−6	+1
Ratio of Change	−	.69	.62	.56	.69	.63	.58	.56	.54	.59	.46	.62	.53

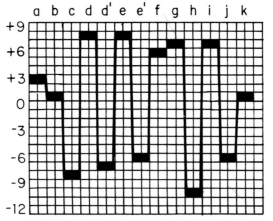

Fig. A.6. Mozart, "Confutatis" (Photo 10).

− +	a	b	c	d	e	f	g
grave/acute	∓	Ø	∓	−	+	−	−
centered/extreme	+	−	+	−	−	+	+
narrow/wide	+	−	+	−	−	+	−
compact/diffuse	∓	−	∓	−	−	−	−
non-spaced/spaced	∿	∿	∿	∿	∿	∿	∿
sparse/rich	+	−	+	−	−	−	−
soft/loud	+	−	+	−	−	−	−
level/oblique	∿	∿	∿	∿	∿	∿	∿
steady/wavering	∿	∿	∿	∿	∿	∿	∿
no-attack/attack	+	−	+	−	−	−	−
sustained/clipped	∓	−	∓	−	−	∓	−
beatless/beating	∿	∿	∿	∿	∿	∿	∿
slow beats/fast beats	∓	−	∓	−	∓	−	−
Neutral (Ø)	0	1	0	0	0	0	0
Negative (−)	2	10	2	11	9	8	10
Mixed (∓)	4	0	4	0	1	1	0
Positive (+)	7	2	7	2	3	4	3

Totals

$$\begin{bmatrix} -4, & -8, & -4, & -9, & -8, & -7, & -8, \\ +9 & +0 & +9 & +0 & +2 & +3 & +1 \end{bmatrix}$$

| +5 | −8 | +5 | −9 | −6 | −4 | −7 |

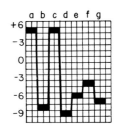

Fig. A.7. Berlioz, "Tibi omnes angeli" (Photo 11).

	− +	a	b	c	d	e	f
grave/acute		−	+	∓	+	∓	∓
centered/extreme		−	+	+	−	+	+
narrow/wide		−	−	+	+	+	+
compact/diffuse		−	−	−	−	−	∓
non-spaced/spaced		−	−	+	−	−	−
sparse/rich		−	−	−	+	+	+
soft/loud		−	Ø	Ø	Ø	+	+
level/oblique		−	−	−	−	−	∓
steady/wavering		−	+	+	+	+	+
no-attack/attack		−	−	−	−	+	+
sustained/clipped		−	−	−	∓	∓	∓
beatless/beating		−	+	+	+	+	+
slow beats/fast beats		Ø	−	−	∓	∓	∓
Neutral (Ø)		I	I	I	I	O	O
Negative (−)		12	8	6	5	3	I
Mixed (∓)		O	O	I	2	3	5
Positive (+)		O	4	5	5	7	7

Totals
$$\begin{bmatrix} -12, & -8, & -7, & -7, & -6, & -6, \\ +0 & +4 & +6 & +7 & +10 & +12 \end{bmatrix}$$

	-12	-4	-1	0	+4	+6
Ratio of Change	−	.46	.42	.49	.52	.57

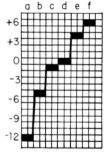

Fig. A.8. Debussy, "Nuages" (Photo 12).

− +	1	2	3	4	5	6	7	8a	8b
grave/acute	Ø	∓	∓	∓	∓	∓	∓	−	−
centered/extreme	−	+	+	+	+	+	−	+	+
narrow/wide	−	+	+	+	+	+	+	∓	∓
compact/diffuse	−	−	−	−	∓	∓	−	−	−
non-spaced/spaced	−	−	−	−	−	−	+	−	−
sparse/rich	−	−	+	+	+	+	−	−	−
soft/loud	−	−	Ø	+	−	−	−	−	−
level/oblique	∼	∼	∼	∼	∼	∼	∼	∼	∼
steady/wavering	−	+	+	∓	∓	∓	∓	−	+
no-attack/attack	−	−	−	−	∓	∓	−	∓	∓
sustained/clipped	−	−	−	−	∓	∓	−	∓	∓
beatless/beating	−	+	+	+	+	+	+	+	+
slow beats/fast beats	Ø	−	∓	∓	−	−	−	−	−
Neutral (Ø)	2	0	1	0	0	0	0	0	0
Negative (−)	11	8	5	5	4	4	8	8	7
Mixed (∓)	0	1	2	3	5	5	2	3	3
Positive (+)	0	4	5	5	4	4	3	2	3

$$
\text{Totals}\begin{bmatrix} -11, & -9, & -7, & -8, & -9, & -9, & -10, & -11, & -10, \\ +0 & +5 & +7 & +8 & +9 & +9 & +5 & +5 & +6 \end{bmatrix}
$$

	1	2	3	4	5	6	7	8a	8b
	-11	-4	0	0	0	0	-5	-6	-4
Ratio of Change	—	.50	.46	.39	.54	.43	.44	.54	.47

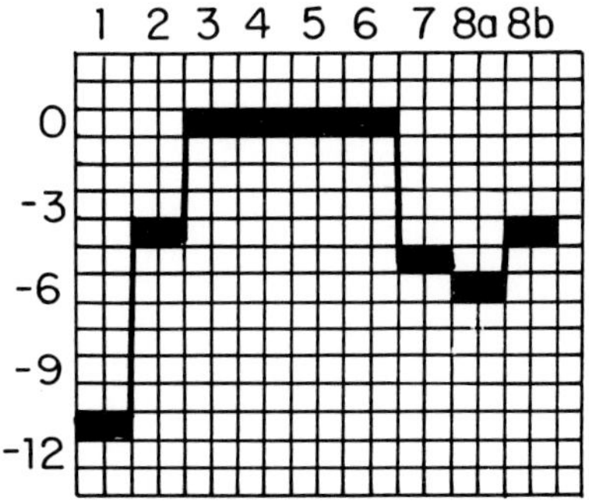

Fig. A.9. Edgard Varèse, *Hyperprism* (Photo 14).

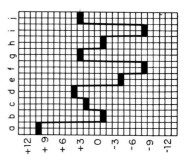

	a	b	c	d	e	f	g	h	i	j
grave/acute	+	−	∓	∓	−	−	∓	∓	+	∓
centered/extreme	+	+	+	+	+	−	+	+	−	+
narrow/wide	+	−	+	+	−	−	+	+	−	+
compact/diffuse	+	+	−	∓	∓	−	−	∓	−	∓
non-spaced/spaced	+	−	−	−	−	+	−	−	−	−
sparse/rich	+	−	+	+	−	−	+	+	−	+
soft/loud	+	∓	+	+	∅	−	+	+	−	+
level/oblique	∓	∓	∓	∓	∓	∓	−	∓	−	∓
steady/wavering	∓	∓	−	−	−	−	−	∓	+	∓
no-attack/attack	+	+	−	∓	∓	−	+	+	−	∓
sustained/clipped	∓	∓	∓	∓	∓	−	∓	∓	−	∓
beatless/beating	+	+	+	+	+	+	+	+	−	+
slow beats/fast beats	+	−	+	+	−	−	+	∓	∅	∓
Neutral (∅)	0	0	0	0	1	0	0	0	1	0
Negative (−)	0	5	4	2	6	10	4	1	10	1
Mixed (∓)	3	4	3	5	4	1	2	6	0	7
Positive (+)	10	4	6	6	2	2	7	6	2	5
Totals	[−3, +13] +10	[−9, +8] −1	[−7, +9] +2	[−7, +11] +4	[−10, +6] −4	[−11, +3] −8	[−6, +9] +3	[−7, +6] −1	[−10, +2] −8	[−8, +12] +4

Fig. A.10. Jean-Claude Risset, "Fall" (Photo 16).

− +	a	a'	b	c
grave/acute	−	∓	∓	∅
centered/extreme	+	+	+	−
narrow/wide	−	+	+	−
compact/diffuse	−	−	−	+
non-spaced/spaced	−	+	−	−
sparse/rich	−	−	+	+
soft/loud	−	+	∓	−
level/oblique	+	+	∓	+
steady/wavering	～	～	～	～
no-attack/attack	～	～	～	～
sustained/clipped	−	−	∓	−
beatless/beating	−	−	+	+
slow beats/fast beats	∅	∅	∓	−
Neutral (∅)	1	1	0	1
Negative (−)	10	6	4	8
Mixed (∓)	0	1	5	0
Positive (+)	2	5	4	4

Totals
$$\begin{bmatrix} -10, & -7 & -9 & -8, \\ +2 & +6 & +9 & +4 \end{bmatrix}$$

	a	a'	b	c
	-8	-1	0	-4
Ratio of Change	—	.36	.68	.70

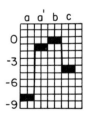

Notes

Introduction

    1. Igor Stravinsky, *Poetics of Music*, tr. Arthur Knodel and Ingolf Dahl (Cambridge, Mass.: Harvard University Press, 1947), p. 27.

    2. Ludwig Wittgenstein, *Philosophical Investigations*, tr. G. E. M. Anscombe (New York: Macmillan, 1953), p. 36e.

    3. R. H. Van Gulik, *The Lore of the Chinese Lute* (Rutland, Vt.: Tuttle, 1968), pp. 99–139.

    4. Charles M. Bakewell, *Source Book in Ancient Philosophy* (New York: Scribner's, 1907), p. 60.

    5. Robert Cogan and Pozzi Escot, *Sonic Design: The Nature of Sound and Music* (Englewood Cliffs: Prentice-Hall, 1976).

    6. Roman Jakobson and Linda Waugh, *The Sound Shape of Language* (Bloomington: Indiana University Press, 1979).

    7. Hermann von Helmholtz, *On the Sensations of Tone*, tr. A. Ellis (New York: Dover, 1954; after the 2nd English ed., 1885), chs. 4–6.

    8. Language sounds within brackets are to be read according to international phonetic practice.

    9. Ernst Mach, "Zur Analyses der Tonempfindungen," *Sitzungsbericht Kaiserlich Akademie Wissenschaft* (1885), class 92, pt. 2, pp. 1283–89.

    10. On the basis of my studies of the role of spectral elements in sonic structures, I assigned first-order significance to spectral presence or absence, and second-order significance to loudness gradation of spectral elements. My observations suggested that sets of neural on-off responses (with a threshold requirement) predominate in the auditory system, rather than entirely graded ones. Only one of the seventeen analyses presented here (Photo 9) required a thoroughgoing spectral loudness representation in order to understand its sonic transformations. When first-order factors do not suffice to shed light on a particular context, I then went to second-order factors.

    11. Ralph Potter, George Kopp, and Harriet G. Kopp, *Visible Speech* (New York: Dover, 1947).

    12. Hermann Broch, *The Sleepwalkers*, tr. Willa and Edwin Muir (New York: Grosset and Dunlap, 1947), p. 398.

    13. Harvey Fletcher, *Speech and Hearing in Communication* (Princeton: Van Nostrand, 1953). Fletcher et al., "Quality of Piano Tones," *Journal of the Acoustical Society of America* 34 (1962): 749–761; idem, "Quality of Organ Tones," ibid. 35 (1963): 314–325; idem, "Quality of Violin, Viola, 'Cello and Bass-Viol Tones," ibid. 37 (1965): 851–863.

14. Cogan and Escot, *Sonic Design*, ch. 4.

15. Edgard Varèse, "The Liberation of Sound," in Elliott Schwartz and Barney Childs, eds., *Contemporary Composers on Contemporary Music* (New York: Holt, Rinehart & Winston, 1967), p. 196.

16. "Nature has provided music with one—and only one—prototype." Oswald Jonas, *Introduction to the Theory of Heinrich Schenker*, tr. and ed. John Rothgeb (New York: Longman, 1982), p. 15.

17. "German melody, the true melody of music, is the total melody of this synthesis. In contrast other peoples lack, with few exceptions, the musical power and perseverance to produce similar structures and spans. Their melody is an end-in-itself of only a fleeting moment, immature, infertile for synthesis however beautiful the moment might be." Heinrich Schenker, *Das Meitsterwerk in der Musik*, vol. 1 (Munich: Drei Masken, 1925), p. 205. All translations are my own unless otherwise noted.

18. Claude Lévi-Strauss, *The Savage Mind* (Chicago: University of Chicago Press, 1966), p. 38.

19. "Can you lend me the [Goethe] *Theory of Colors* for a few weeks? It is an important work." *Ludwig Van Beethovens Konversationshefte*, Karl-Heinz Köhler and Grita Herre, eds., vol. 9 for the year 1820 (Leipzig: Deutscher Verlag für Musik, 1972), p. 348. "The most sublime book of all time," wrote Webern to Alban Berg on September 28, 1929; quoted in Hans Moldenhauer, *Anton Webern* (New York: Knopf, 1979), p. 328.

20. See John Gage, *Color in Turner* (New York: Praeger, 1969), p. 11.

21. Vincent Van Gogh, *Van Gogh*, letters selected by W. H. Auden (New York: Dutton, 1963), pp. 217, 319–320.

22. Johannes Itten, *The Art of Color* (New York: Van Nostrand Reinhold, 1960). On Pope, see Howard Fisher and James Carpenter, *Color in Art: A Tribute to Arthur Pope* (Cambridge, Mass.: Fogg Art Museum, 1974).

23. Leonard Slatkes, *Vermeer and His Contemporaries* (New York: Abbeville, 1981), pp. 8, 11–12.

1. Voices

1. *Sources of "Qui sedes, Domine." Recording:* Music Guild MS-137, *Gregorian Chants. Score: Liber Usualis*, edited by the Benedictines of Solesmes (Tournai: Desclee, 1963), pages 335–336. Since the recording transposes the chant approximately a whole tone lower than the *Liber Usualis* notation, the notation here has been transposed to correspond to the spectrum photo of it.

2. Brian Cutillo and Nga Wang Lek Den, trs., "The Invocation of Mahakala," in notes to the recording *The Music of Tibet: The Tantric Rituals*, Anthology AST-4005.

3. Peter Crossley-Holland, "The Music of the Tantric Rituals of Gyume and Gyuto," ibid.

4. Kenneth Stevens, "Description of the Mode of Chanting," ibid.

5. Crossley-Holland, "The Music of the Tantric Rituals."

6. Philip Rawson, *Tantra* (London: Thames & Hudson, 1973), pp. 8–9.

7. *Sources of Invocation of Mahakala. Recording:* Anthology AST-4005, *The Music of Tibet: The Tantric Rituals. Score:* The notes to the recording include a copy of the original graphic notation.

8. William Vennard, *Singing: The Mechanism and the Technique* (New York: Carl Fischer, 1967), pp. 89–90.

9. *Sources of "Strange Fruit."* *Recording:* Verve V-8505, *The Essential Jazz Vocals.* Photo 3 omits the applause and brief piano introduction; the limited interpolations of the piano appear only in a few isolated notes at the end of line 1. *Score:* Billie Holiday and Lewis Allan, "Strange Fruit," composed 1938 (New York: E. B. Marks).

10. Quoted in Ove Nordwall, *Gyorgy Ligeti: Eine Monographie* (Mainz: B. Schott's Söhne, 1971), p. 78.

11. Rainer Wehringer, *Ligeti Artikulation* (Mainz; B. Schott's Söhne, 1970), p. 11.

12. Gyorgy Ligeti in notes to the recording *Requiem, Lontano, and Continuum,* Heliodor (Wergo) 2549-011.

Sources of Lux Aeterna. Recording: Deutsche Grammophon Gesellschaft 137-004. *Score:* Gyorgy Ligeti, *Lux Aeterna,* for mixed chorus of sixteen voices (Frankfurt: Litoff/Peters, 1966). *Readings:* Gyorgy Ligeti, "Metamorphoses of Musical Form," tr. M. Shenfield, in *Die Reihe,* vol. 7 (Vienna: Universal Edition, 1960), pp. 5–19; Ove Nordwall, *Gyorgy Ligeti: Eine Monographie* (Mainz: B. Schott's Söhne, 1971); Rainer Wehringer, *Ligeti's "Artikulation": An Aural Score* (Mainz: B. Schott's Söhne, 1970).

2. Instruments

1. Anne Chatoney Shreffler, "Baroque Flutes and Modern: Sound Spectra and Performance Results," *The Galpin Society Journal* 36 (March 1983): 88–96.

2. In *Music in Bali,* Colin McPhee describes the complex distribution of the strata of shadow-play music between the two players of the *gendèr* pair in the *gendèr wayang* ensemble; see McPhee, *Music in Bali* (New Haven: Yale University Press, 1966), pp. 202–204. He observes that the music is reproduced an octave higher by a second pair of *gendèr.* This account, he says, is "based on the version played by the *gendèr wayang* of Kuta village." On page 218 he adds that "this last part of the *Pemoengkah,* as played by the Kuta ensemble, was recorded on Odeon." Photo 5 reveals that the Kuta village recording used only a *single* pair of *gendèr* without octave doublings, and that McPhee was misinformed about the size of that ensemble. Had the higher-octave pair of *gendèr* been present, the spectral content of registers 4 and 5 would be reproduced an octave higher in registers 5 and 6, and the spectral gap in those registers correspondingly reduced (see Photo 5 and commentary). Comparison with other *Pemoengkah* recordings confirms these conclusions. When the larger ensemble is used, some spectral activity appears in the gap in register 6. But more spectral elements high in registers 7 and 8 are added, so that the spectral concentrations and morphology are not essentially different from the description in Chapter 2.

The octave doublings also appear in the two-piano version in Colin McPhee, *Balinese Ceremonial Music* (New York: G. Schirmer, 1934). Performers should realize that a number of measures from the first and last parts of the original composition are omitted in that transcription, significantly altering the proportions.

3. "Great attention is paid to trimming each resonator to the exact length at which it will produce an air column vibrating in unison with the key above. Tones of great purity and fine resonance result, and in the larger instruments the resonators prolong the tones to an astonishing extent." McPhee, *Music in Bali,* p. 31.

4. *Sources of Pemoengkah. Recording: Music from Bali,* Tape 2, available from

the Archive of the Institute of Ethnomusicology, University of California, 405 Hilgard Avenue, Los Angeles, California 90024. This is a tape of the 1928 Odeon recording that McPhee used as reference. *Transcriptions:* Colin McPhee, *Music in Bali*, pp. 219–222. This is an incomplete sketch transcription of an entire *Pemoengkah*, including parts of the excerpt discussed here. Also, Colin McPhee, *Balinese Ceremonial Music*, for two pianos, four hands.

5. *Sources of Piano Sonata in E Opus 109. Recordings:* BASF (Harmonia Mundi) KHF-20328, *Beethoven's Clavier;* Jörg Demus, fortepiano. Seraphim IC-6065, vol. 4, Ludwig Van Beethoven, *Piano Sonatas;* Artur Schnabel, piano. *Score:* Ludwig Van Beethoven; Piano Sonta in E Opus 109, 1820 (Vienna: Neue Beethoven Edition). Good reprints of this sonata are available in editions by Henle, Universal Edition, and others.

6. Already in 1913 Debussy wrote of Stravinsky's "sonorous magic." Letter of April 10, 1913, reprinted in Robert Craft and Igor Stravinsky, *Conversations with Igor Stravinsky* (Garden City: Doubleday, 1959), p. 51. Ten years later this was amplified by Erik Satie: "One of the characteristics of Stravinsky's music is its transparency of sound. You will certainly be struck by the amazing sharpness with which you can discern this 'clearness' of vibration. The whole of his 'orchestra' is based on instrumental timbre." *The Writings of Erik Satie* (London: Eulenburg, 1980), pp. 104–105.

7. Edward T. Cone, "Stravinsky: The Progress of a Method," *Perspectives of New Music* 1 (Fall 1962): 18–26.

8. Robert Cogan and Pozzi Escot, *Sonic Design: The Nature of Sound and Music* (Englewood Cliffs: Prentice-Hall, 1976), pp. 276–284. Also Robert Cogan, "Stravinsky's Sound: A Phonological View," *Sonus* 2 (Spring 1982): 15, 20.

9. William Innes Homer, *Seurat and the Science of Painting* (Cambridge, Mass.: MIT Press, 1964), esp. p. 64.

10. *Sources of Three Pieces for String Quartet, Piece II. Recording:* Everest 3184, *Homage to Stravinsky. Score:* Igor Stravinsky, *Three Pieces for String Quartet,* composed 1914 (New York: Boosey and Hawkes).

11. Igor Stravinsky, "Foreword," *Die Reihe,* vol. 2 (Vienna: Universal Edition, 1955), p. 7.

12. *Sources of Four Pieces for Violin and Piano, Pieces III and IV. Recording:* Columbia M4-35193, Anton Webern, *The Complete Works,* vol. 1. *Score:* Anton Webern, *Four Pieces for Violin and Piano,* Opus 7, composed 1910 (Vienna: Universal Edition).

13. Robert Cogan, "Tone Color: The New Understanding," *Sonus* 1 (Fall 1980): 18.

14. Elliott Carter, "On the Double Concerto," in Robert Stephan Hines, *The Orchestral Composer's Point of View* (Norman: University of Oklahoma Press, 1970), p. 49.

15. *Sources of Eight Etudes and a Fantasy, Etude III. Recording:* Etude III, performed by the New England Conservatory Scholarship Woodwind Quartet (Stephanie Jutt, flute; Sandra Apeche, oboe; Ian Greitzer, clarinet; Richard Sharpe, bassoon), prepared by John Heiss and Robert Cogan. Other performances are available on commercial recordings. *Score:* Elliott Carter, *Eight Etudes and a Fantasy,* for woodwind quartet, composed 1950 (New York: Associated Music Publishers). The performance above was chosen for its unusual faithfulness to the score; however, see p. 71.

3. Large Mixed Ensembles

1. Friedrich Blume, "Requiem But No Peace," *Musical Quarterly* 47 (1961): 147.

2. See the remarks of Nikolaus Harnoncourt in notes to his recording of the Requiem, Telefunken 6-42756.

3. *Sources of Requiem K. 626, "Confutatis." Recording:* RCA AGLI-1533, Wolfgang Amadeus Mozart, *Requiem K. 626.* A recording of the Requiem using original instruments, with boys' voices instead of women's and purged of Süssmayr's instrumental additions, is now available: Pro Arte 1026, performed by the Collegium Aureum. It came to my attention too late to be photographed and used in this book. It does not alter the conclusions presented here in any important respects. *Score:* Wolfgang Amadeus Mozart, *Requiem K. 626,* composed 1791 (Vienna: Neue Mozart Ausgabe). This edition shows all of the essential aspects of the "Confutatis" known to have been composed by Mozart and indicates those aspects that were the contribution of F. X. Süssmayr, a student of Mozart who completed the composer's score.

4. *Sources of Te Deum, "Tibi omnes angeli." Recording:* Philips 839-790-LY, Hector Berlioz, *Te Deum. Score: Te Deum,* Opus 22, composed 1849 (London: Bärenreiter).

5. Quoted in Jean Barraqué, *Debussy* (Paris: Editions du Seuil, 1962), p. 106.

6. Ibid.

7. Ibid.

8. Robert Cogan and Pozzi Escot, *Sonic Design: The Nature of Sound and Music* (Englewood Cliffs: Prentice-Hall, 1976), pp. 393–397.

9. In Photo 12, between Stages 1 and 2, there is an instant that foreshadows all of the coming transformations in the piece. We will not consider it further here.

10. Its entire set of notes, B^3–F^4, stands exactly midway between the outer extremities of the movement (F^1 and B^6) and reproduces the same boundary notes, B and F.

11. *Sources of "Nuages." Recording:* Crossroads 22-15-0091, Claude Debussy, *Nocturnes.* This recording, unfortunately, is no longer available. It is perhaps the most accurate and beautiful of the many recordings of this work, including the more recent one also conducted by Fournet, as well as those by better-known conductors. *Score:* Claude Debussy, *Nocturnes,* composed 1899 (New York: International Music). Bärenreiter will soon publish this in their new critical edition of Debussy's works. Its appearance will be welcome, for there are important discrepancies in the scores and performance traditions of this work.

12. Alban Berg, "Lecture on *Wozzeck,*" in H. F. Redlich, *Alban Berg: The Man and His Music* (New York: Abelard-Schuman, 1957), p. 281.

13. Willi Reich, *Alban Berg,* tr. C. Cardew (New York: Harcourt, Brace & World, 1965), p. 140.

14. *Sources of Wozzeck. Recording:* Columbia M2-30852, Alban Berg, *Wozzeck. Score:* Alban Berg, *Wozzeck,* Opus 7, composed 1922 (Vienna: Universal Edition), pp. 417–418.

15. Edgard Varèse, "The Liberation of Sound," in Elliott Schwartz and Barney Childs, eds., *Contemporary Composers on Contemporary Music* (New York: Holt, Rinehart & Winston, 1967), p. 196.

16. Ibid., p. 198.

17. Ibid., p. 197 and passim.

18. Ibid.

19. *Sources of Hyperprism. Recording:* Angel S-36786, *Music of Varèse. Score:* Edgard Varèse, *Hyperprism,* composed 1924 (New York: Franco Colombo, Inc.).

4. Electronic and Tape Music

1. *Source of Ensembles for Synthesizer, Introduction. Recording:* Columbia MS-7051, Milton Babbitt, *Ensembles for Synthesizer.* I am indebted to Wayne Slawson for first noticing the analytic challenges of this work.

2. Pierre Halet, *Little Boy.* See notes to the recording *Voice of the Computer,* Decca DL-710180.

3. Roger N. Shepard, "Circularity in Judgments of Relative Pitch," *Journal of the Acoustical Society of America* 36 (December 1964): 2346-53. Shepard's illusion can be heard on *Voice of the Computer,* Decca DL-710180.

4. *Source of Little Boy, "Fall." Recording:* Decca DL-710180, *Voice of the Computer.*

5. Quoted in Victor Navasky, "E. L. Doctorow: 'I Saw a Sign,' " *New York Times Book Review,* Sept. 28, 1980, p. 44.

6. Quoted in Alma Mahler, *Gustav Mahler: Memories and Letters,* tr. Basil Creighton (New York: Viking, 1946), p. 94.

7. Igor Stravinsky and Robert Craft, *Dialogues and a Diary* (Garden City: Doubleday, 1963), p. 79.

8. From notes to the recording *No Attack of Organic Metals,* Delos DEL-25445.

9. When spectral elements are close enough to form beats, the speed of the beats (in bps) equals the difference of the frequencies of the two spectral elements (in Hz).

10. *Sources of No Attack of Organic Metals. Recording:* Delos DEL-25445, *A Sonic Experience with Martha Folts at Harvard. Score:* unpublished; available from the composer.

5. The Theory of Oppositions

1. These analyses are to be found in Robert Cogan and Pozzi Escot, *Sonic Design: The Nature of Sound and Music* (Englewood Cliffs: Prentice-Hall, 1976), ch. 4 and Postlude. Also in Robert Cogan, "Tone Color: The New Understanding," *Sonus* 1 (Fall 1980): 3–24.

2. Maurice Merleau-Ponty, *The Primacy of Perception* (Evanston: Northwestern University Press, 1964), p. 180.

3. Roman Jakobson and Linda Waugh, *The Sound Shape of Language* (Bloomington: Indiana University Press, 1979).

4. "The linguistic values of sounds to be examined by phonology are abstract in nature. They are above all *relations, oppositions, etc.*" N. S. Trubetzkoy, *Principles of Phonology,* tr. C. A. M. Baltaxe (Berkeley: University of California Press, 1969), p. 13.

5. Jakobson and Waugh, *The Sound Shape of Language,* p. 3.

6. Trubetzkoy, *Principles of Phonology,* p. 31.

7. Karl Jaspers, *The Great Philosophers,* vol. 2 (New York: Harvest, 1966), p. 5.

8. Ibid., p. 12.

9. For phonological tables of oppositions, see Roman Jakobson, C. Gunnar,

M. Fant, and Morris Halle, *Preliminaries to Speech Analysis* (Cambridge, Mass.: MIT Press, 1951), pp. 43–45.

10. Jakobson and Waugh, *The Sound Shape of Language*, p. 19.

11. A spectrum photo of the Introduction is reproduced in *Sonus* 2 (Spring 1982): 1–2.

6. Specific Oppositions

1. N. S. Trubetzkoy, *Principles of Phonology*, tr. C. A. M. Baltaxe (Berkeley: University of California Press, 1969), pp. 72–73.

2. Ludwig Wittgenstein, *Philosophical Investigations* (New York: Macmillan, 1953), prop. 88, pp. 41e–42e.

3. Roman Jakobson and Linda Waugh, *The Sound Shape of Language* (Bloomington: Indiana University Press, 1979), p. 13.

4. See Robert Cogan and Pozzi Escot, *Sonic Design: The Nature of Sound and Music* (Englewood Cliffs: Prentice-Hall, 1976), the analyses of Debussy's "Nuages" and Schoenberg's "Farben," pp. 385–397 and 412–426.

5. For an explanation of sone measurement, see Harvey Fletcher, *Speech and Hearing in Communication* (Princeton: Van Nostrand, 1953), pp. 189–194.

6. See Chapter 4, note 9.

7. Parenthetical Issues

1. Wayne Slawson, "The Color of Sound," a paper read to the Society for Music Theory (Denver), November 7, 1980.

2. Both quotations appear in Karl Popper, *Objective Knowledge* (Oxford: Oxford University Press, 1972), p. 135.

3. Roman Jakobson and Linda Waugh, *The Sound Shape of Language* (Bloomington: Indiana University Press, 1979), p. 21.

4. Quoted ibid., p. 27.

5. Ibid.

6. E. L. Saldanha and J. F. Corso, "Timbre Cues and the Identification of Musical Instruments," *Journal of the Acoustical Society of America* 36 (1964): 2021–26.

7. N. S. Trubetzkoy, *Principles of Phonology*, tr. C. A. M. Baltaxe (Berkeley: University of California Press, 1969), pp. 4–12, 12–13.

8. This is not the place to explore all of the similarities and differences between music and language as sonic structural systems. The greatest possible difference is that language derives considerable meaning as a signifier, referring beyond itself, whereas musical functions are largely, but not entirely, self-referential. In the light of recent work demonstrating the power of self-referential processes (work by Bateson, Hofstadter, and others) as well as work that conceives of music as an information system or as a generative grammatical system (work by Hiller, Jackedoff and Lerdahl, Lewin, Meyer, Pierce, Powers, and others), I would caution against an uncritical exaggeration of this *possible* difference. It seems to me that better than the *a priori* assumption of differences is the open-minded exploration of structural principles for their explanatory value. After that explanatory power has been explored, and not before, much more will be apparent about the similarities and differences. This book is offered as an instance of such a pragmatic, exploratory approach.

9. Jürgen Meyer, *Acoustics and the Performance of Music* (Frankfurt/Main: Verlag Das Musikinstrument, 1978), pp. 50–51.

8. Archetypes

1. Robert Cogan and Pozzi Escot, *Sonic Design: The Nature of Sound and Music* (Englewood Cliffs: Prentice-Hall, 1976), pp. 276–284. Also Robert Cogan, "Stravinsky's Sound: A Phonological View," *Sonus* 2 (Spring 1982): 15, 20.

2. Edward T. Cone, "Stravinsky: The Progress of a Method," *Perspectives of New Music* 1 (Fall 1962): 18–26.

Conclusion

1. Gregory Bateson, *Mind and Nature* (New York: Bantam, 1979), p. 122.

Index

Acoustics, 4, 21
Albers, Josef, 19
Allen, Lewis, 35
Anaximander, 125
Apollinaire, Guillaume, 121, 147
Archetypes of sonic transformation, 147–152
Attack noise, 48, 56, 60, 61, 65, 85, 87, 90, 138, 139, 143, 145, 147. *See also* Onset
Audible range of humans, 7–8, 14, 147, 156
Audio equipment, 13, 27

Babbitt, Milton: *Ensembles for Synthesizer*, 103, 104–108, 126–129, 131–132, 148, 150
Bach, Johann Sebastian, 78
Balinese gamelan music, 44, 104; *Pemoengkah*, 45–49, 133, 149, 159
Bassoon, 90, 91
Bateson, Gregory, 153
Beats, 48, 49, 90, 114, 118–119, 135, 136, 139–140, 141, 142, 147
Beethoven, Ludwig van, 2, 3, 6, 15, 18, 44; Piano Sonata in E, Op. 109, 44–45, 49–56, 144
Bell Laboratories, 14, 16, 96, 108
Berg, Alban: *Wozzeck*, 2, 3, 6, 11, 73, 92–96, 128–129, 148, 149
Berlioz, Hector: Te Deum, "Tibi omnes angeli," 73, 80–85, 148–149, 151, 152, 162
Boulez, Pierre, 92

Camera oscura, 19
Carter, Elliott: *Eight Etudes and a Fantasy*, Etude III, 45, 66–72; *Eight Etudes and a Fantasy*, Etude VII, 66

Cézanne, Paul, 123
Chinese description of sound, 1
Choral effect, 139
Clarinet, 90, 91, 135, 136
Cogan, Robert: *Sonic Design: The Nature of Sound and Music*, 16, 87; *No Attack of Organic Metals*, 103–104, 112–119
Color (visual), 3, 6, 18–19, 21, 87, 92; complementary colors, 19, 58
Computer, 5, 16, 108, 111
Cone, Edward, 58, 149
Corboz, Michael, 74

Davis, Colin, 80
Debussy, Claude, 45; Nocturnes, "Nuages," 73, 85–92, 104, 148, 149, 150–151, 152, 163
Delacroix, Eugène, 18
Democritus, 4
Demus, Jörg, 49, 52, 53
Density, 33, 58–61, 62, 64, 65, 66, 76, 85, 87, 90, 91, 96–101, 102, 126, 135–137
Details of spectrum photos, 10, 13–14, 31, 47, 59, 67–69, 88–89, 117, 136, 138, 155, 156
Doctorow, E. L., 112
Dynamics, 15, 126, 137, 155

Electromechanical sounds, 112, 113, 114, 119
Electronic music, 16, 103–119, 145
English horn, 89, 92
Escot, Pozzi, 5, 16, 58, 87

Fletcher, Harvey, 16, 17, 96
Flute, 44, 48, 70, 71, 81, 97, 101, 113, 145–146
Folts, Martha, 112

Formants, 25–26, 27, 42, 76, 79, 84
Fortepiano, 45, 49–56, 144
Fournet, Jean, 85
Franz, Helmut, 39
French horn, 84, 93, 101, 102

Gendèr, 44, 45–49, 133
Goethe, Johann Wolfgang von, 19, 21
Gombrich, E. H., 142
Gregorian chant: "Qui sedes, Domine," 21–28, 35, 42, 111, 148, 149, 157

Hegel, Georg Wilhelm Friedrich, 125
Helmholtz, Hermann von, 9, 11, 12, 14, 15, 16, 18, 123, 145
Heraclitus, 125
Hertz, Heinrich Rudolf, 6
Holiday, Billie, 2, 3, 6, 15, 23; "Strange Fruit," 35–38, 42

Impressionism, 1, 18
Itten, Johannes, 21

Jakobson, Roman, 4, 124–125, 126, 133–134, 143

Language sounds. *See* Linguistics
Lévi-Strauss, Claude, 18
Ligeti, Gyorgy: "Lux Aeterna," 23, 39–43, 148, 158
Light, 3, 6, 18, 21, 39, 142
Line (music), 27–28, 37, 76–77, 124
Linguistics (and language), 3, 4, 5, 9, 14, 15, 16, 23–28, 35–43, 74–85, 124–125, 133–134, 143–146; vowels, 4, 9, 10, 12, 14, 25–28, 32, 37, 38, 39, 41, 42–43, 74, 76, 79, 81, 84; phonology, 5, 14, 23, 125, 133, 144–145, 146, 153; consonants, 11, 14, 17, 32, 33, 39, 138; phonetics, 23, 43, 144–146
Loudness, 15, 45

Mach, Ernst, 12
Mahler, Gustav, 112
Matisse, Henri, 19
Maxwell, James Clerk, 18
McPhee, Colin, 45, 49
Merleau-Ponty, Maurice, 123–124
Messiaen, Olivier, 136
Monet, Claude, 18
Mozart, Wolfgang Amadeus: Requiem, "Confutatis," 73, 74–80, 111, 148, 161

New England Conservatory Scholarship Woodwind Quartet, 66
Noise spectra, 11, 43, 47, 64, 85, 87, 95, 96, 113, 135
Notation, 29, 35, 103, 119, 137
Note bending, 35–38

Oboe, 70–71, 72, 91, 93, 95
Onset, 60–61, 137–138, 145
Oppositions, 3, 27–28, 29–35, 41–43, 54–56, 56–61, 62, 71, 73, 74, 78, 80, 81, 84, 85, 91, 95–97, 101, 106, 111, 116, 119, 123, 124–132, 133–140, 142–143, 144, 147, 150, 153, 157–165; grave/acute, 12, 27–28, 29, 32–35, 37–38, 42–43, 52, 56–61, 72, 74, 78–80, 81–84, 101–102, 106–108, 111–112, 125, 126, 133, 134–135, 145, 152; level/oblique, 32, 35, 137, 151; sparse/rich, 32, 33–35, 60–61, 62, 64, 87, 90, 95, 97–101, 126, 135–137, 139, 145; narrow/wide, 60, 78, 87, 90, 96, 101–102, 107, 126, 133, 135, 145, 152; soft/loud, 60, 85, 96, 101, 133, 137, 151; sustained/clipped, 60, 138–139, 145; centered/extreme, 90–92, 106–107, 134–135, 145, 152; no-attack/attack, 96, 137–138, 143, 145–146; compact/diffuse, 96–101, 135, 136, 137, 138, 139, 140, 151, 152; nonspaced/spaced, 135–136, 152; steady/wavering, 137, 143; beatless/beating, 139; slow beats/fast beats, 139–140
Orchestration, 27, 42, 85–87, 143, 152
Organ, 81–85, 90, 103–104, 112–119, 148
Overtones. *See* Partials

Parrenin String Quartet, 56
Partials, 9–14, 17, 25, 29, 33, 35, 47, 55, 64, 65, 66–70, 74, 90, 108, 135, 136
Peirce, Charles Sanders, 124–125
Percussion instruments, 29–35, 45–49, 73–74, 85, 87, 91, 95–102, 151
Phoneme, 126, 133, 143
Piano, 2, 3, 7, 8, 13, 14, 44–45, 49–56, 62–66, 144, 145. *See also* Fortepiano
Pissarro, Camille, 18

Plato, 125
Popper, Karl, 142

Ratio of change, 127, 128, 129–131, 150–152
Recording, 15, 16, 19
Registers: numbering of, 7–8; display of, in spectrum photos, 12–13; low-register elements, 13
Risset, Jean-Claude: *Little Boy*, "Fall," 2, 3, 6, 103, 108–112, 148, 152, 165
Rosen, Charles, 62
Rothko, Mark, 19

Saint-Saëns, Camille, 129
Satie, Erik, 45
Schenker, Heinrich, 17
Schnabel, Artur, 15, 49, 52, 53
Seeger, Charles, 14
Seurat, Georges, 18, 58
Shakuhachi, 138, 142, 145
Shepard, Roger: Shepard's tones, 108–110
Silence, 58–60, 61, 95, 138–139
Simonovitch, Konstantin, 96
Sine tone, 7, 9–11, 12, 13, 91, 93, 113, 136
Singer's formant, 38
Slawson, Wayne, 141
Sliding motion (glissando), 29, 32, 34, 35, 60, 137. *See also* Note bending; Oppositions, level/oblique
Sonic change: local and global, 129–132, 148, 150–152
Sonic character: negative, positive, neutral, or mixed, 126–129, 132, 147–152
Sonic direction. *See* Sonic character
Sound spectrum: defined, 9–12; harmonic spectrum, 11, 13
Sound spectrum analyzer, 4, 8, 142, 155–156

Sound waves, 6–7, 104, 141
Speech sounds. *See* Linguistics
Stern, Isaac, 62
Stevens, Kenneth, 29
Stratification, 48–49, 58, 61, 149–150
Stravinsky, Igor, 1, 45, 72, 113; *Three Pieces for String Quartet*, Piece II, 56–61, 149, 152, 160; *Le Sacre du Printemps*, Introduction, 129–130, 148
Süssmayr, F. X., 74

Tables of oppositions, 125–132, 133, 134, 147, 153, 157–165
Thomson, Alexander, 143
Tibetan Tantric chant: Invocation of Mahakala, 13, 23, 28–35, 104, 133
Time, in spectrum photos, 8, 13, 14–15, 141–142, 155
Trombone, 74, 95, 102
Trubetzkoy, N. S., 125, 133, 144
Trumpet, 95, 104, 145
Turner, J. M. W., 18, 19

Van Gogh, Vincent, 19
Varèse, Edgard, 17; *Hyperprism*, 73–74, 96–102, 104, 148, 164
Vermeer, Jan, 19
Vibrato, 81, 90, 137, 143
Violin, 62–66, 74, 87, 93, 142, 143

Waugh, Linda, 124, 126, 133, 143
Webern, Anton, 45, 58–60, 72; *Four Pieces for Violin and Piano*, Opus 7, Pieces III and IV, 62–66
Wehringer, Rainer, 43
White noise, 136
Wittgenstein, Ludwig, 1, 133
Woodwinds, 45, 73, 74, 81, 84; woodwind quartet, 66–72

Young, Thomas, 18